Searching for God

by

CARDINAL GEORGE
BASIL HUME, O.S.B.

HODDER AND STOUGHTON

LONDON SYDNEY AUCKLAND TORONTO

First published September 1977
Second impression November 1977
Third impression November 1977
Fourth impression December 1977
Fifth impression March 1978
Sixth impression May 1978
Seventh impression August 1978

Contents

5

6   CONTENTS

Acknowledgments

I am indebted to several persons for my being able to publish the following conferences which as Abbot of Ampleforth I delivered there to the monastic Community.

Fr. Geoffrey Lynch, O.S.B., for the benefit of those who were unable to be present, typed out the original conferences in their entirety.

The selection in this book, taken from an accumulation of conferences extending over a period of thirteen years, was compiled by Fr. Felix Stephens, O.S.B., who also arranged the order, provided the titles, and handled the business side of the enterprise.

To Elizabeth Hamilton, author of several distinguished biographies, including *Cardinal Suenens*, fell the task of transposing the language into a rather more formal style, better suited to the written as distinct from the spoken word. In this she has been skilful and painstaking—without her help the book would not have seen the light of day!

Fr. Barnabas Sandeman, O.S.B., has read the text more than once and made many valuable suggestions. And I must not forget Abbot Herbert Byrne, O.S.B., Abbot of Ampleforth 1939–63, and Abbot President of the English Benedictine Congregation, from whom, I am happy to acknowledge, I, like so many others, received so much. Now aged ninety-three, he still continues to exercise his priestly ministry at the Benedictine parish of St. Mary's Leyland, Preston.

To these and to all my monastic brethren I have much for which to be grateful.

G.B.H.

Introduction

The 'desert' and the 'market place'.

In the monastic world of the West there has always been a tension between the two. Is the monk a person who withdraws into the desert to pray and be alone with God, or is he someone who goes out into the market-place to mingle with and serve the people? This tension, I believe, exists in most communities of Black monks—as distinct, for example, from the Cistercians and Carthusians. To some extent it exists in every English Benedictine monk. Moreover it is a problem which the monk himself must learn to resolve, but also one which each community has from time to time to consider and make such adjustments as seem appropriate.

The conferences assembled here reflect to some degree this tension. And it is arguable that it is not altogether an unhealthy one, for in each of us, deep down, it results from the Christian attempt to respond to the twofold command to love both God and our neighbour. The Gospel requires that the Christian should be constantly seeking God. This presupposes a desire for silence and solitude in order to discover the reality of God's love for us; but equally the Christian must seek to find Christ in his neighbour and to serve Christ in his neighbour's needs.

I gave these conferences between the years 1963 and 1976, when I was Abbot of Ampleforth. They were years of great change. The Vatican Council in its decree on the religious life, *Perfectae caritatis*,[1] requires that religious should go back to their origins to rediscover the spirit of their founders and study how these can be relevant to the needs of the modern world. A daunting task. Strictly speaking, monasticism as such did not have a 'founder'. The monastic 'thing' is not confined

[1] P.C. section 2.

11

to Christianity. Indeed the Rule of St. Benedict was not an original composition nor, until the time of Charlemagne, was it the only rule for monks in the West. In recent years the question has often been asked: 'What is a monk?' In my view no tidy definition can be given—only a broad assessment, sufficiently embracing to cover a wide variety of monasteries in lands of different cultures and varied histories. But the question is a fair one. I make the point here only to explain that these conferences reflect the kind of debate that has been going on in all monastic communities since the Council, and which, to a large extent, remains unresolved. To look at one particular community wrestling with this or that problem may provide support and consolation to others.

The monastic community to which these conferences were given has several diverse pastoral responsibilities: a large boarding school, a university house of studies, a number of parishes, a foundation in the United States and a Retreat house. All this apart from individual calls on the time and energy of the monks to preach Retreats, give conferences or just be available to their fellow-men in good times and bad. It is a busy life which inevitably has its problems. The main one is the task of keeping a balance between the three essential ingredients of monasticism: prayer, work, and community life. Prayer and work must clearly be closely related; pastoral work will be successful in the true and deepest sense only if the monk is a man of prayer.

The monks of the English Benedictine Congregation have, on the whole, always been involved in pastoral activities. The reasons why they have been so involved are in the main historical: this is not the place to tell that story.

The ideal monastic community, it is also worth noticing, does not exist. Any such community is made up of very ordinary men from different backgrounds, with different ideas and ideals. This can make the life of the monk interesting and creative. It is also the reason why the Rule of St. Benedict is so understanding. For the Abbot there is no better guide on the art of ruling a community than the principle which St. Benedict enunciates in chapter 64 of the Rule, where he writes that the monastery should be so organised that the strong always have something to strive after, while the weak are not weighed down by burdens too crushing to bear.

The Rule of St. Benedict tells the Abbot that he must be a teacher who is able to put before his monks things old and new. The reader will notice that at Ampleforth the Abbot himself had to grapple with a variety of problems in an effort to reconcile the old and the new as the latter were presented by theologians and monastic thinkers. Indeed certain of the things he said in 1963 he may have wished to modify in 1976. The master continues to be a disciple. Some of the early conferences are included in this collection. It is for the reader to judge whether the monastic doctrine of those early years can be defended in the years that follow. If it stimulates thought and reflection it will have served its puɪpose.

There were two occasions in particular when conferences were given: the weekly conference, normally on a Tuesday night at nine p.m. (not a good time either for the speaker or the listeners!), and the special monastic 'moments' when the Abbot was required to speak to his monks. This was known as a 'Chapter'.

A word about the special 'moments'. After an eight-day Retreat the prospective monk is 'clothed' as a novice. He receives the habit in the presence of the whole Community and the Abbot gives a talk. A year later the novice takes vows for two years or three. On the eve of the ceremony (sometimes known as 'making Simple Profession') the Abbot speaks to the novice or novices, again in the presence of the Community. Between the 'clothing' and 'Simple Profession' there are three what are known as 'Perseverances'. After three, six, and then nine months the novice's progress in the novitiate is considered at some depth; the Novice Master reports to the Abbot's Council and the Council then agrees (or does not) to allow the novice to continue in this way of life. The novice is 'granted Perseverance' and is told so before the whole Community by the Abbot, who once again gives a talk. The novice kneels in front of the Abbot, but the words spoken by the Abbot, it has sometimes been said, are also addressed to the rest of the Community in the choir stalls. There is some truth in this. After four or five years the monk makes his 'Solemn Profession' (that is, he takes his vows for life), and the same routine as the Simple Profession obtains. Each year the Community assembles for the Annual Conventual Chapter. All the monks renew their vows and on this occasion, too, the Abbot addresses them.

The monk commits himself by a vow to the search for God and his service. He binds himself by three vows. The vow of stability attaches him to a particular community for the rest of his life. Although the monk may be sent to engage in any work which is the responsibility of the monastery in question he always remains a member of that same monastic family to which he has first committed himself. The vow of obedience commits him to accept the directives of his Superiors, but from the monk's point of view it is also his way of expressing his intent to seek always the will of God in that monastery. The third vow which he takes, known in Latin as *conversio morum*,[1] is perhaps best translated by 'conversion of manners'. It is not easy to explain exactly what this means, but in general terms it can be said that the monk undertakes to lead a life of a certain kind which includes such values as celibacy, frugality, and simplicity, and in general to embrace those characteristics of monastic living which have been constant throughout the history of monasticism.

Strictly speaking, a monk's life is not organised for any particular work or service in the Church. His main purpose is to seek God and this he takes on as a life-long task. In a sense this is no different from the task of any Christian or indeed any person. The monastic life is simply one way of leading the Christian life and this the monk does in a community. The value of a monastery within the Church is principally the fact that it exists. It is a spiritual centre which should give witness to the things of God and be a place which draws to itself for spiritual refreshment and encouragement those who have a different vocation. The life of the monk obviously differs in many respects from that of persons

---

[1] *Conversio morum* a phrase which has long confused interpreters of the Rule, but means in essence, a daily turning of the heart to God and a way of life in accord with the spirit of monasticism.

who have a different calling. The principles which guide the monk in his search for God and the Gospel values, which he tries to make his, are relevant to both Christians and non-Christians alike. This is perhaps the only justification for hoping that persons other than monks may find something to help them in this book.

G. B. HUME
February 1977

PART ONE:

Monastic Life and Work

I

Man and God

1. Religious Instinct

I WOULD LIKE to reflect with you tonight upon man as a religious being, and upon an aspect of the liturgy which seems to me to be closely associated with that.

Man, I am convinced, is religious by nature. The religious instinct belongs to his very nature, is part of his make-up. It is part of his make-up to be orientated towards God. True, for the vast majority of persons this orientation is unknown, unrecognised. Often it is directed towards things that are less than God; but in so far as the mind is constantly groping towards the ultimate meaning of things and in so far as man's desire craves to be satisfied by this or that good, then the unacknowledged, unrecognised, unknown search for God has begun. Many indeed of man's frustrations are attributable to the fact that he cannot, and does not, in his present condition, attain that ultimate in knowing and that ultimate in loving which belong, so it seems, to the very perfection of his nature. And in so far as he fails to attain it either in the realm of his knowing or in that of his loving, to that extent he remains a frustrated being.

His Christian life depends, in the first instance, on something outside himself, because it is primarily and fundamentally a response to a particular historical situation: a response to an event, to the Incarnation and all that follows from that—and ultimately to the Resurrection. As I see it, the religious instinct is a fact of my nature: it is inside me. The Christian response, however, being in the first place a response to an event, is from that point of view outside me. It is the Christian 'thing' which gives meaning to and ultimately fulfils the religious instinct, because it is Christ who is the way, the truth, the life, and in him we find the ultimate reasons for things and the ultimate love for which our nature craves.

I believe also that every man is a hidden Christian. And in two senses. Man is saved by Christ, in that only through Christ can he attain the beatific vision. And furthermore, all yearnings for the divine, whatever form they take, are and must be attributed to the Holy Spirit. That is at one level. But man is also a hidden Christian because, although he is not in a situation in which he is consciously responding to Christian values — in all probability he does not know Christ and will not have heard of these values — there is nevertheless something of Christ in him, as in everyone. And there are many senses, I think, in which this is true. The most obvious, the most simple, is the fact that Christ became man. The fact that he shared our human condition gives significance to every human life wherever it is, whatever it is, and whatever religious belief is held.

In becoming man, Christ became all men.

It would be easy to say that the religious instinct is something that belongs to nature — is natural — and that the Christian 'thing' is gratuitous — belonging to grace — and therefore supernatural. I often go back in my thinking to this distinction between man as a religious animal and man as a Christian, with the provisos I have stated — namely, the importance of seeing every man ·as a hidden Christian. I prefer 'hidden' Christian to 'potential' Christian, because I think that 'potential' is too weak. 'Hidden' is better because our pastoral task is to draw out the Christ who is within a person, so that this Christ within may grow to the full stature of Christ as he should be in every individual.

Let us revert to the religious instinct. What are its characteristics? One is a sense of awe: awe when confronted with something greater than 'self'. Instinctively men realise that there is something greater than they are. In man's entire religious experience this has been so. This 'intuition' was brilliantly described by St. Anselm. I call it an 'intuition', not an 'argument', because the argument which St. Anselm used about the existence of God is not convincing as such — it was not so much an argument as an intuition.

Another characteristic of the religious instinct is a

sense of bafflement in the face of the unknown: an awareness that all things have an ultimate meaning which the mind cannot grasp, yet is always seeking. This is very much the basis of that aspect of mystical theology which one associates with the 'Cloud of Unknowing'. Then there is the sense of wonder: a constituent of the religious instinct and stemming from the aesthetic experience which is the capacity to appreciate and respond to the beautiful. It is—to paraphrase some words of C. S. Lewis—the power to detect shafts from the glory of God as they impinge upon our sensibility.

Secular man would say—indeed, does say—that these feelings of awe, wonderment, a sense of the unknown, are primeval instincts which are bound up with fear, with the need for security, with the search for a father-figure, and with a primitive desire to escape from the dark, and so on. Much of this I find true. But it is one thing to say this is what we are like, and quite another to discover a reason—and it requires to be discovered— why we are like this, why we have these instincts, what they signify. These are the questions which need to be answered.

If I am right in saying that the religious instinct is strong in man and can easily be awakened, and if one of its constituents is wonderment stimulated by aesthetic experience, then we are justified in underlining a particular aspect of the liturgy—and it is only one aspect. The liturgy should always contain within it the beautiful, because beauty is one of the means by which we are led to God. A beautiful thing speaks to us of God. What we love in any creature is only what is a reflection of God. It is the beautiful which can arouse in us wonder, can lead us to a response which is not exclusively rational—and rightly so, in that we are not simply rational beings, but so much more. The liturgy therefore should sometimes and in some circumstances deliberately speak to us of God through beauty. And beauty as a constituent of the liturgy will be one of the things that activates the religious instinct; it will also be one of the means whereby this instinct will find expression. It is important that there should be a decorum, an order, a rhythm. It is indeed saddening that so much we do is not done well. The liturgy

Beauty in the liturgy . . .

should be adapted to different circumstances, different moods. Intimacy and simplicity are proper to small groups. On other more formal occasions the emphasis should be on beauty, respect, awe, wonderment.

A 'little dread' . . .

May I add a little footnote? One of the things I have often noticed in the last four or five years, when I come back to Ampleforth after being away, is a 'little dread' inside me.

We have acquired the habit (this is not peculiar to us, it is the times we live in) of being over-critical. People are tensed up. Everything is controversial, divisive. It is exhausting, and not a good sign. I don't know that we can do much about it except laugh. You know, it is quite astonishing to go back and stay in a family for a little bit and then return here and find people all tensed up, rather like springs! We all need to relax and to criticise things without getting worked up. The trouble focuses itself around the liturgy—the one thing in which we ought to find pleasure and joy. (The devil is a clever fellow!) We need to be less 'strung-up' and then, I think, we shall be more recollected, more prayerful, and more charitable.

26. 1. 71

2. Monastic Instinct

I have for some time been cast down at the thought of my inadequacy as a monk. My shortcomings take different forms. Sometimes I am a bit 'easy-going'; at others what I can only call a bit 'worldly'. When I am either, the spine goes out of my prayer life and there is a loss of sensitivity in my response to God. It is rather embarrassing if an abbot makes an act of confession in public. I do it solely to show solidarity with others who perhaps have the same feeling.

What is meant by being 'worldly'? It is hard to say. Also it is a mistake to try to analyse the concept too closely and get lost in a whirl of theory about what the 'world' means or what one's rôle should be. What I am talking about is really a monastic instinct, clearly recognisable in those who have it. It is a kind of instinct by which one is able to judge what is fitting for a monk and what is not. This can cover a wide spectrum of activity, attitude, speech, the way we pass our holidays, how we spend money, the kind of hospitality we give, the kind we receive, our behaviour, things we say, our values. There is no end to it.

Not all of us have this monastic instinct, and not all of us, if we think we have, live up to it. There is, however, an awareness, within reach of us all, as to what is fitting and what is not. On the other hand, if you point out things that seem unfitting for a monk it is not always easy to give a reason: it is just an instinct. There are two words (we used them in the past, and they are still the best) which describe what should be the monastic attitude to the world. They are frugality and simplicity. Moreover it is worth adding that we must not allow ourselves to be deceived into thinking that being 'in the swim' is going to be important or give us influence. At schoolmaster level, for example, that would be a ludicrous mistake—a mistake that is made, nonetheless.

Others should find us easy, approachable, warm, but they should detect something else. It is a 'something else' built up through years of fidelity, striving, having one's treasure elsewhere. Personally I do not like, in the matter of relationships with the outside world (going out for meals, popping in for a drink and so on) to lay down hard-and-fast rules. But some people prefer it that way because they like things clear-cut—indeed the easiest way to run a monastery is to have a lot of rules! But we do need to have norms, such as: 'We do not go out for supper'; 'We only go out to lunch with relations of the first degree of consanguinity.' The norm must be there, but there will be and ought to be exceptions and special circumstances. The tidiest, neatest way is to say: 'That is the rule, that is the way it is.' But I do not think this is Benedictine. I do not think it accords with such principles as: 'Let him so temper all things that the strong may still have something to aim at and the weak may not draw back in alarm.'

I do not believe that in a Benedictine monastery all should be treated alike. And let me add—though it may seem a bit over-defensive—I do not think Superiors should necessarily be consistent. The onus is very much on the individual to know when to ask and when not to. 'There is no harm in asking,' is the comment of a schoolboy, not an adult. This is not intended as an attempt to 'tighten up', but rather to help us to pick our way over a very difficult area and to impress on us all, myself included, the importance of frugality and simplicity. The tendency to take things easy is part of the make-up of each one of us.

What I am trying to say is that we should each of us recognise our responsibility and thus cultivate what I call a 'monastic instinct'. For not only can the spine go out of our prayer life: the entire community can lose its spine.

To conclude, let me remind you of the Prologue in which St. Benedict talks of establishing a school of the Lord's service where, he says, 'we hope to ordain nothing that is harsh or burdensome, but if for good reason, for the amendment of evil habits or the preservation of charity, there be some strictness of discipline, do not at once be dismayed and run away.'

The phrase 'amendment of evil habits' is harsh, but we should understand it in the sense of not allowing ourselves to become easy-going.

'The preservation of charity.' That is profound. For a high standard in monastic life we all depend on mutual encouragement and example. Indeed, encouragement and example, to which I would add enthusiasm, are elements which keep a community buoyed up: encouragement to one another, an example to one another, and a general enthusiasm for all that we are and all that we do. The greatest abnegation of self, indeed (to go a step further) the most characteristic way of living chapter 2 of the Epistle to the Philippians is to be able to throw oneself into the monastic life and work with enthusiasm in this age when self-criticism and questioning can dispose us to become insufficiently involved. There is something here of great importance upon which each one of us should ponder: to deny ourselves and throw ourselves into what is going on, whole-heartedly and enthusiastically, even when we have mental reservations: this, I would say, is a *kenosis*, a self-emptying. And it is this quality which is, I think. demanded of us in the Church today.

12. 6. 73

II

Monastic Formation

1. Ceremony of Clothing

To learn: about God, self, community

RECENTLY I WENT to see one of our Community who
has begun to lead the life of a hermit. He does not
know, and neither do I, whether this is the life to
which God is calling him. It will take time for him
to find out. And without a doubt he will have to go
through periods of aridity and difficulty if he is to
become a hermit in the true sense. His present novitiate,
as far as we are concerned, is based on no experience.
We go forward tentatively, hesitantly. When he and I
discuss his life, it is novice talking to novice.

In training young men for the monastic life—allowing for human imperfections—we know, by and large,
what we are doing. Yet you resemble this novice in
that you are here to discover whether this is the life
God wants for you. And we, the Community, are here
to help you, guide you, teach you. For your part you
should see this year—at any rate from one point of
view—as a period of retreat during which you will
have to learn many things, the chief one being how to
seek God—not as a hermit, alone, but in community.

First, you have to learn about God. And you will
find that it is, above all, in prayer that the Christian
seeks to meet God. Today we badly need men and
women who can talk with conviction, based upon
whatever experience God is pleased to give them, about
God himself, Father, Son, and Holy Spirit, and the
love which is the explanation of the Trinitarian life,
finding its correlative in the explanation of the Christian
life. Like the rest of us, you are here, in the words of
St. Benedict, to seek God.

25

Secondly, you will have to learn about yourselves. I wonder whether, as we go through life, we ever know ourselves as we really are. How often we hide behind an image we like to have of ourselves and certainly would like others to have of us. But you will have to learn about yourselves, if you are to discover what is displeasing in the sight of God and what is difficult for those with whom you have to live. Only in this way can you correct your faults, make necessary adjustments. Your strength lies in the talents God has given you. See them more and more as gifts from him, which, when you make your profession, you will give back to him.

Life in the novitiate will be circumscribed and the things you will be given to do will be, in the eyes of men, small, unimportant, and frankly rather dull. That can be irksome. But learn, learn in the first week, that everything you do and everything that happens to you must be seen as an opportunity to deepen your love of God; that everything you do and everything that happens to you is to be enjoyed, or suffered, whichever it may be, with and through Christ. You are seeking God in community and you will soon discover what joy it is to live in community; what support you get from sharing with others the same ideals, the same aspirations, the same way of life. And community life is always a joy if you live unselfishly, if you control the itch to be self-assertive and are determined not to seek your own will. When someone is unhappy in community it is in these areas that he needs to examine himself.

Living in community... And you will have to learn how to live in community. You will not find, in this Community, unanimity of opinion on any subject; on some you will find profound differences. You may be surprised how we differ. But you will also be surprised at how united we are. And the sooner you become, in every sense, one of us, the better for you and indeed for us. It is one thing to live with people you yourself have chosen: it is another to live with those who happen to be there when you arrive. It is one thing to live with people of a like mind, another to live with those of a different outlook. This is one reason why novices are cut off from the rest of the life of the community: because you need to learn quickly how to live, day in and day out, in a restricted group. If you can do that, you can live, believe me, with anyone.

Throughout his Rule St. Benedict warns his monks *Murmuring...* against the vice of murmuring. It is important to be critical in one sense, but not in the sense that, when you find things are not to your liking, this will upset you and cause you to grumble. There is a good, constructive way of criticising; but there is also a bad way, and that is what St. Benedict is talking about. You will learn from your experience how easy it is to be destructively critical; to be over-hasty in making judgments, to be intolerant of the faults of others, their ignorance, short-sightedness, lack of vision.

Ours is a great life, a great vocation, and in it you will find joy and peace: a peace which no man can take from you. I shall end with quotations from two mystics. The first is: 'If dark clouds would hide you from my gaze so that it seemed that after this life there was only a night darker still, the night of utter nothingness, that would be the hour of greatest joy, the hour in which to push my confidence to its uttermost limits.'[1] And the other: 'Strike the thick cloud of unknowing with the sharp dart of yearning love and on no account whatsoever think of giving up.'[2] The first was written in the 1890s, the second in 1370. I would like to think that these might provide you with a motto for your novitiate:

Confidence: a boundless trust in God's goodness.
Yearning love: the love for God which is the point of
    the monastic life.

And finally, don't take yourselves too seriously. Take *life* seriously. Take *God* seriously. But don't, please don't, take yourselves too seriously!

6. 9. 69

To explore: the mystery which is God

From the very beginning try to penetrate to the heart

[1] *St. Thérèse of Lisieux*: Autobiography, chapter 13.
[2] *Cloud of Unknowing*, trans. Walters, Penguin 1961, chapter 6, p. 60.

of your vocation. It is easy, especially in the early years, to hold a mistaken view of what a monk's perfection consists in.

Monastic life is not, in the first place, the pursuit of virtue; it is not, in the first instance, the keeping of rules; it is not, primarily, a theological debate or reflection, nor is it involvement in social action nor the pursuit of hard work. All these have their part, but any one of them can be erected into an idol, turning things that are means into ends or absolutes.

What, then, is at the centre of our monastic calling? An exploration into the mystery which is God. A search for an experience of his reality. That is why we become monks. The exploration is a life-long enterprise. And when we come to the end of our lives our task will not have been completed. Such experience as God will grant you will be a limited, pale thing compared to that for which we are ultimately destined.

Even in the earliest years of the monastic life you can be distracted from your purpose. You can become preoccupied, say, with the acquiring of virtue and miss the whole point. You will realise, I think, that when I talk of the monastic life as an exploration into the mystery that is God, what I am really saying is that it is on our part a response to an initiative that rests entirely with him. The fact that you are kneeling here in the presence of our Community is no more than a first step in your response to an invitation which both you and we ourselves believe to have been extended to you.

To hear and to see . . . The attitude a monk must have throughout his life, if his exploration is to be real and his search effective, is one of listening and looking. You must pray daily that the Spirit of God—the power of Christ—will open your ears and cure your blindness so that in all situations and events you will be able to hear God's voice and see, in whatever befalls you, something of himself. In proportion as you listen and look you will find reason for praising him and giving him thanks; and to praise and give him thanks is something we do several times a day here in this choir. And so when St. Benedict talks of the qualities a novice should have, he puts first the necessity of discovering whether he is zealous for the work of God. Moreover the qualities listed are demanded not only of the novice but of every monk throughout his entire life.

The second quality for which St. Benedict asks is that the novice be obedient. The Latin word *obedientia* derives from one which has to do with 'hearing', 'listening'. Obedience, for St. Benedict, is very much a matter of the attitude or relationship existing between a master and his disciple. In your first year you are here to learn the ways of God. You will be instructed by your Novice Master, and also by the Rule.

The Rule of St. Benedict was a codification over a period of time of an experience lived. Similarly, a monastic community is a living community with its own collective experience. You must observe the Community—listen and look; discover its spirit and why people act as they do; their motives in staying. From all the monks you can learn something that will be of value to your vocation. As learners you are under a discipline. You are disciples. Be sensible about rules: they are means not ends, but important means. Do not take them too lightly, as of little account. Your guides in this matter are your Abbot, your Prior and your Novice Master: they are your lawfully constituted authorities. Follow their guidance.

St. Benedict requires that a novice should accept *Opprobria...* *opprobria*. The word means disgraces. It is normally translated 'humiliations'—which is scarcely more cheerful. What it really amounts to is this: can a novice be told things about himself without his being unduly hurt, ruffled, or put out? In short, is he humble? It is not all that easy. Even late in life you discover with dismay that humiliations are not easy to accept. Face the fact that you will be told many things; embrace this fact and profit from it.

St. Benedict goes on to say that the difficulties on our path to God should be put before the novices. Now one of the greatest of these is the apparent absence of God. I shall be surprised if within the next twelve months you do not at some time or other experience this. It is one of the greatest trials we undergo in a monastery. It is, of course, at these moments that we seek an escape—into work, into social life: any number of escape routes are available. Let me remind you that when you feel God's absence, Christ our Lord, our model and our hope, experienced just this. There is a rhythm of light and darkness. Happily the memory of light enables us to support the darkness, to look forward to the re-emergence of light. For there *is* light, and plenty of it. It comes by the initiative of God himself. Our task is to be faithful, to persevere, to respond. In proportion as we give, in proportion as we commit ourselves, in proportion as we pray and are humble, in proportion as we draw closer to God, he will bless us and guide us.

17. 1. 73

To listen: to the wisdom of the Master

'Listen, my brothers, I have something to tell you. I have a way of life to teach you. Listen to me with an open heart and mind. If you follow my instructions obediently and faithfully, you will find him who is the source of all your desires, the very one you have bypassed by going your selfish way.'

These, roughly translated, are the opening words of the Rule of St. Benedict. You have come to this monastery, and you must begin in the conviction that, whatever your faults, whatever the difficulties that may ensue, however obsolete our structures may seem, you can, each one of you, attain what you are seeking. You can and will, if you persevere, discover God.

The opening word of the Rule is 'Listen'. That must colour your whole approach, not only this year but throughout your lives. You are learning here and now how to be a disciple the whole of your lives. The confined circumstances of life in the novitiate may puzzle you. You may have your own ideas as to how a novitiate should be run. Yet ours is a well-tried manner of approach.

Your function is threefold. First, you have to get to know God and him whom he has sent: Jesus Christ our Lord. With this in view we provide you, in the novitiate, with a 'desert', so that without preoccupations other than those traditional in a novitiate, you will have the opportunity to pray, read, and reflect. It is a golden opportunity.

Secondly, you have to get to know yourself, and there

will be little chance of escaping. You have to face up to what you are; and the discovery may be disconcerting, even alarming.

Thirdly, you have to get to know one another. You have to learn how to live together—to learn the art of community life, with patience, tolerance, generosity, and respect. You would be a curious lot if you did not at some time in the course of the year get on one another's nerves. And remember, if someone else is getting on your nerves, you are almost certainly getting on his. You will have to learn how to face that kind of situation in the charity of Christ. This knowledge of God, yourself, and your neighbour should lead you to a threefold loving: a love of God, of yourself, and of the brethren.

A disciple is one who listens. If the lesson is to be valuable, you have to be receptive—receptivity is very much a quality we expect from a novice. You have everything to learn about the ways of God. It is not easy today. The world is in a state of flux. So is the Church. Questions are being asked. There are uncertainties. But do not forget that wherever you are, with whomsoever you are, whatever you are doing, you can, in the present moment, attain union with God. We are all inclined to think that if circumstances were other than they are, things would be better. Do not be too sure. It is in the depths of our hearts that we meet God, and nothing can separate us from his love.

A word about humility. It is not only a virtue, it is a basic attitude, and a Christian one which makes for a good and an attractive human being. Perhaps a better word than humility is freedom: internal freedom. Freedom from what? Freedom from being self-seeking, self-regarding, self-indulgent, self-opinionated. None of us is humble enough. But let me break off a moment on an excursus to cheer you up! All the monks here are in some way wounded. You are joining a community composed of extremely imperfect human beings. It is rather like being in a hospital where the matron, as well as the patients, is sick! You are not entering a community of saints. If that is what you thought we were, then please go before I clothe you! No, we are very human, and it is important to remember this. We need to be freed from our self-seeking, from the wrong kind of ambitions, from conceit, from being trapped within our limitations, from thinking we are right and others wrong—all that kind of thing. We need to be freed. Free for what? Free to find him who, as the Rule says, is the 'source of all our desires': free to love—you cannot love unless you are free.

Be free to love your neighbour: in the first instance, your brethren. And this means treating one another with respect, reverence, restraint. That kind of freedom which, as I have suggested, is to be equated with humility, will be the basis of your happiness, your cheerfulness, and will protect you from the worst of all monastic faults—what, as I have said, St. Benedict calls murmuring: murmuring, grumbling, being always critical—critical of persons, of how things are done, continually voicing your criticisms, being unable to accept decisions, being 'put out'. That kind of thing is pernicious. I beg you not to be grumblers. If you want to be humble, free, detached; if you are seeking God, wanting him alone, then cheerfully (God loves a cheerful giver) and good-naturedly you will be able to achieve great things for and within the Community.

We are all, I said, to some extent wounded. You remember the words in the Gospel: 'It is not those who are in health who need the physician, but those who are sick.' Ponder long and often on God's love for you and his mercy. Remember the paradox: 'To live you have to die.' 'Give and you will receive.' 'Lose and you will find.' 'Die and you will live.' 'Obey and you will be free.' The more free you are, the more you will want to obey. That is why, for St. Benedict, obedience is linked closely with humility.

19. 1. 74

2. Perseverance

Safe in the market-place because at home in the desert

I would like to say something about the rôle of the desert and that of the market-place in monastic life— particularly life as lived in this monastery.

By the desert I mean withdrawal from activity and

people to meet God. By the market-place I mean involvement in pastoral situations of one kind or another. The tension between the two is a constant in the whole monastic tradition, and monastic history is a commentary on that tension. Should we be in the desert, withdrawn, or should we be in the market-place, involved? St. Augustine, talking about bishops, says that while love of truth drives a man to seek holy leisure, the demands of charity, require his involvement: *Otium sanctum quaerit caritas veritatis, negotium justum suscipit necessitas caritatis.*[1]

Reform in the monastic life is always in the direction of the desert, because the 'pull', the attraction of the market-place, carries with it its inherent dangers, making a monk or a monastery forgetful of the values of the desert. That tension which we find throughout monastic history exists, I believe, in every monastery — indeed, in every monk — the 'pull' within each one of us between wanting to withdraw and wanting to be involved. The art of being a monk is to know how to be in the desert and how to be in the market-place. That is why in our monastic life we provide, in terms of time and place, a desert — that is, a desert situation — where silence is precious, silence required.

We are foolish when we think in terms of rules of silence, as if these were an external discipline imposed because monastic life should have discipline. Rather, we should see these places and times of silence as the very basis of a mature, adult spiritual life. We should not see silence as an interruption of our recreation; we should see our recreation as punctuating our silence. But the desert has to be something in the mind, and it is the appreciation and understanding of the rôle of solitude and internal silence — and the relationship between that inward attitude and the exterior means which we provide for ourselves — that enable us to acquire, or to dwell in, the internal desert of solitude and silence. Those times and places of silence are refuges to which we withdraw because we want them, because we need them, because it is there we seek God.

Now the market-place is distracting. Of itself it has attractions, and in it we find responsibilities to be

[1] St. Augustine, *De civitate Dei 19, No. 19.*

3

carried out. We can, too, escape to the market-place because we fear the desert, because we are fearful of solitude, fearful of silence; because we are fearful to face the demands and claims which God might make, indeed does make, upon us. *We shall never be safe in the market-place unless we are at home in the desert.* That is why the early years in the novitiate are of vital importance; because the novitiate is an attempt to create a desert situation; its absence from occupation, its lack of human contacts, have precisely this purpose: that we may discover the claims and demands God is making upon us. You may smile when I talk of lack of occupation, but you understand what is meant. The lack of contacts—apart from those with whom one shares the novitiate—presents problems; and in that context let me revert to the theme of the desert and leave with you one thought. The heart, too, must learn to live in its desert if it is to be capable of involvement in the market-place. It is only in the desert that you can learn to turn loneliness into solitude, and it is only when we have learnt solitude and freedom—the capacity to be alone—that we can safely be involved with others.

Our monastic life here is in the market-place: we have a school, parishes, the Grange.[1] Some of us are involved with administration. That is our life. That is the way history has forged us. That, it seems, is God's will for us. And because we are involved in the market-place it is crucial for us to appreciate the desert. A monk is valuable in the market-place if he preserves a nostalgia for the desert: a nostalgia to be a man of prayer, leisure for prayer, the desire for prayer—hanging on to this, never letting go; this it is which fits us for God's call to be involved with people and activity. Quite simply, our life is one of prayer and service in community, and we live it, with its contradictions and complexities, much in the spirit of the Rule of St. Benedict. To live happily together, to attain the aims each sets before himself at his profession, we must be a disciplined community, valuing the fundamental doctrines of St. Benedict. And two of these concern humility and obedience. Treasure both. I have read tonight: 'Prayer is the sum of our relationship with God. We are what we pray. The degree of our faith is

[1] Monastic Guest House for visitors and groups making a Retreat

the degree of our prayer. Our ability to love is our
ability to pray.' To this I would add: genuine love of
God and man is learnt in the desert. Learn it there
and you will have something to sell in the market-place
— the pearl of great price.

16. 10. 73

Lowliness

There are many forms of prayer, some suited to some
temperaments, some to others. The Holy Spirit blows
where he wills. But I want to talk about a form which,
because it is intimately bound up with the whole
monastic search for God, ought to be specially treasured: the prayer of quiet.

This prayer, whether it be for five minutes or half
an hour, dispenses with words, images, and ideas. Yet
that does not mean that these have to be totally excluded.
What matters is that we acquire the capacity to be
silent in the presence of God: that we cultivate a silent
awareness in which the soul meets God deep within
itself.

There are different starting points in accordance with *Poverty of*
our way of looking at life, our temperament, reading, *heart ...*
education, and so on. A good one, I would say, is a
consciousness of poverty — what one might call a
radical poverty; or, if you will pardon the expression,
a metaphysical poverty: an awareness of our limitations
as creatures, of the self beyond which lies the nothing
where we encounter God. This awareness of our
poverty in the presence of God awakes a sense of
dependence, enables us peacefully to commend ourselves to God's providence and see in the activity of
daily life his guiding hand.

Another form taken by poverty is a sense of our
inadequacy which makes a continuous claim on God's
mercy — a mercy that, in accordance with the biblical
usage of the word, implies a stooping down of the
greater to uplift the less. 'He that is mighty has magni-
fied me.' Times when we make mistakes or make fools
of ourselves are followed by a deep peace because the
recovery granted to us rests in God. A sense of our
inadequacy, our fragility — which without true faith

leads to a loss of confidence—is, I think, a profound monastic attitude: the realisation that it does not matter how foolish I make myself in my own eyes or in the eyes of others, because I have proved once again how much I need the mercy and help of God. And so this poverty—the poverty of the first beatitude: 'Blessed are the poor in spirit'—is a good starting-point because it is the experience of us all in our prayer life: failure, frustration, seeming to get nowhere. Dwelling on this poverty which presents itself in the difficulties of our prayer, we meet God, or, to be more accurate, we are discovered by God.

This is why humility is a key virtue in the monastic life, a key virtue in the Christian life. This, I think, is why St. Benedict laid such stress on it and in doing so was echoing a whole monastic tradition. He may express the twelve degrees of humility in ways other than we would wish today, but the point to which each leads is the same: the realisation of our poverty and consequently an attitude of mind and a way of behaving in respect of our service of God and our neighbour.

But the silence is and should be a peaceful silence, in which primarily we are listeners. In prayer there is a place for talking, but silence has an all-important rôle. We have only to think of our Lady, the handmaid of the Lord: her lowliness. She 'kept these words in her heart'. She was blessed because she listened to the voice of God. She received the Word, not only physically but into every facet of her being. In such a manner in the prayer of silence, the prayer of quiet, we receive the Spirit.

Pardon me for expressing this clumsily: I admit I do not move very easily in this area; but one has had enough experience to know that it is along these lines that we have to search for a type of prayer which must always be in our monastic life. That is why we have this half-hour of mental prayer. And it is important not to be cavalier about this.

If you can acquire this attitude in the early years of your monastic life it will save you from becoming an 'activist'—in the sense of someone immersed in a hundred-and-one things needing to be done. Moreover this kind of prayer can impregnate whatever we do. As we go about our daily work God is present, as it

were, in the background, enabling us to see Christ in
our neighbour and the divine will in what occupies us.
Or, viewing it somewhat differently, we have a presence
to which we can at any moment return. Hence the
importance of silence: places of silence; deserts where
we can meet God in solitude.   *Silence . . .*

If from time to time you find the Office is not going
well, if it is becoming a bore, I have a couple of tips.
Make it your practice to look forward to the next
Office. Advert to the fact, when going to bed at night,
that within seven hours you will be in choir praising
God in Matins. It is extraordinary what an effect this
little device can have next morning. And it is not a bad
idea to have a special intention for a particular Office,
or a special reason why you want to get up and sing
God's praises that morning. Another thing: find in the
Office of the next day a 'friend' among the psalms.
When the Office is going through a bad patch, a
reading of the psalms is an admirable exercise. We
have to be practical.

5. 7. 73

Obedience

You must feel constricted by the somewhat narrow
life of your novitiate. It is difficult to justify the way
a novitiate is run. There are those now who talk of
what they call an 'open novitiate'. The cynic would
say: 'No novitiate at all!' But it depends on your
starting point. Here, we do not believe in an 'open novitiate', and I cannot see our ever accepting it. It is right,
however, to review from time to time how we do
things in the novitiate and to make necessary adjustments, for one generation of novices will differ from
another. So I hope and pray that our attitude be one
of openness and flexibility. However, as I understand
it, there is no wavering on our part: by and large the
system we hit upon and inherited works; but it is
constricting and confining and there are not many who,
having left the novitiate and become Juniors in the
community, would want to return to the novitiate life.
Yet all of us would wish we had profited more from
our time there.

The important thing in the novitiate is that you should be protected from as many distractions as possible, and this for one reason only—that you should learn to become men of prayer, learn the art of prayer, learn the practice of the presence of God; that you should become 'men of God'. That is the fundamental reason for the whole thing. And I think that if you persevere and later in life look back, you will see, indeed understand, how formative this year can be, or was, or, sadly, was not. In this year the foundations are laid. In this year you have to become 'monks' instead of just living like monks. It is a crucial period. And it is difficult, when involved in it, to understand all this. You are not yet able to look back in retrospect and evaluate it. You are going through a process which is not easy to understand when you are in it; and therefore you need a good deal of patience and a good deal of receptivity to enable you to accept things which on their face value seem to you unimportant or even stupid. Be sensitive to the experience of those who are helping and guiding you. Try to appreciate and understand before you criticise. Don't let your immediate reaction be a critical one: let it be one of appreciation, an attempt to understand. In any monastery, if you look for things to criticise you will find enough to keep you busy all day. If you are sensitive and understanding, then you are in a position to make constructive and sensible suggestions.

It is true that there are many difficulties in what one might call the 'theology of obedience'. It is also true that in the history of the Church, in the history of the religious life, there have been abuses in the exercise of authority. All this has to be admitted. And it is true, I think, that obedience outside the context of the religious life could tend, and sometimes does tend, to diminish the individual. But we have to try to understand why obedience has entered into the spiritual life; why it was important for people like St. Benedict and all spiritual writers down the centuries—this mysterious link forged between our obedience and the obedience of Christ. Sometimes, we are told, obedience is a liberation. It is not always easy to see the meaning underlying this paradox.

May I make two points? If you take a vow of obedience you will lose the freedom to choose what you will do in the monastery. Today more is done on the basis of dialogue and discussion, and authority exercised in a more human way than in the past. Nevertheless you will lose the freedom to choose your own way of life; and this, in itself, is a liberation. Because you accept what is asked of you by your Superiors, you are freed from having to make plans for the future. You are, as it were, a casual traveller through life, rather than one who has worked out his route in advance. You have, of course, to be secure within yourself . . . you have to be certain in your convictions concerning God and the things of God. But the very uncertainty, humanly speaking, as to the future is an encouragement to have trust and confidence in God's providence.

Moreover, obedience is a defence against self-will: no wolf is cleverer at assuming sheep's clothing than the wolf of self-will. What St. Benedict says about this defect sends a chill down the spine. It seems to go against what we call today self-expression, self-fulfil-ment and the rest. But he has a point here. It is easy to make ourselves the centre of our own little universe, to live our lives for our own self-aggrandisement, our own self-gratification. 'Good' people fall into this trap. In their zeal they try to compete with others, trample them underfoot. Do not be so sure that the teaching of St. Benedict on self-will is out of date. Experience shows us how subtly, very subtly, we can seek . . . 'self.' The art of being a Christian and therefore the art of being a monk, is to learn to put God at the centre—the love of God and of our neighbour; to be devoted to God and to our neighbour. You meet people who apparently are very spiritual, very holy—only to detect, on closer acquaintance, that self-seeking takes precedence over seeking God or the service of their neighbour.

5. 12. 69

'. . . a gentle rebuke!'

About the monastic life and those of us who are living it, you know more than you understand. Understanding comes more slowly, trailing behind knowledge.

Knowledge and under-standing . . .

The humble
man . . .

There is no limit to what a humble man can do in the service of God and his neighbour. Conversely, there is no greater obstacle that the reverse of humility: pride. St. Benedict's chapter on humility is a whole spiritual programme.

I have a faint impression — I put it in this way because I may qualify, or you may want to qualify, what I am going to say — I have a faint impression that you entered the novitiate to put us to the test rather than (as is usual in the monastic life) our putting *you* to the test! Now, we don't want you to be uncritical. We don't want you to be 'stuffy'. We don't want to pretend to you that we have all the answers — we haven't, as no doubt you have noticed.

But it is important to remember that if you are really going to learn about the monastic life, there is a good deal which you have to accept on simple trust, believing that it works or is important. Possibly I have put this more strongly than I intended, but we know each other well enough to make all necessary reservations. However, I am not trying to eliminate just a slight rebuke!

Community
life . . .

You have discovered already, haven't you, that eight people living together pose quite considerable problems? It is four times harder than if there are only two of you — I suppose it is easiest if there is only one! But you have discovered the problem! Companions are thrown together whom you have not chosen, and you have not found it easy. It's so simple to talk about community; so simple to think of community as a kind of temporary 'togetherness'. However, when you have to live the life in terms of harsh reality, it poses problems. But you will have discovered your own shortcomings, as far as living in community is concerned. You will also have discovered that it is rewarding, that we derive support from one another. And I think there is evidence that you have learnt a great deal here, and that you are beginning to appreciate each other for what you are and not what you would like others to be. This is a matter of first importance in community living: to take people as they are, not as you would like or expect them to be. A deep tolerance and acceptance of the other — this is the basis of community. After all, it is the basis of charity, to which community is subordinate.

Your novitiate up to this time has been, I would say, *Assessing a*
not an easy one; but it has features that are extremely *novitiate . . .*
encouraging. You are an efficient novitiate, and it is
not often in the past that Abbots have been able to
say this. Yes, by and large you are efficient. That is
not the greatest of virtues; it is not the most important
monastic attribute, but it helps. You are cheerful: that
is important too. And you can, I think, laugh at yourselves — which is very important.

You have two things we treasure. You try to say your
prayers, and in your prayer life you give a good example
to the Community: and that is your most important
quality. You are men with ideals, and that again is
important. Keep to your prayers, keep your ideals,
and all the rest will fall into place.

24. 3. 70

Commitment

There was a time in the monastery here when after one
year of novitiate you took vows for life. And then it
was decided to take vows first of all for three years, at
the end of which time the novice, if he was considered
suitable, was allowed to take his solemn vows. And
when a novice took his simple vows it was on the
understanding that he really intended to remain in the
monastery for life.

Since then, the mind of the Church has changed. A
document from Rome, *Renovationis causam*, makes it
clear that the period of monastic formation extends to
the taking of solemn vows: up to that time you are on
probation. The corollary of this way of thinking is that
we do not contract an obligation to you similar to
those which have hitherto obtained.

Let me explain. Once we have accepted a man for
temporary vows we can only get rid of him — if I may
use this awful phrase — for some serious offence; the
idea being that in accepting him for temporary vows we
virtually accept him for solemn vows. This however is
not the case now. We do not contract the same obligations. In a sense, therefore, you do not have security,
even after two years, because after the two years of
temporary vows your case will be reconsidered. The

Church has decided this in the light of experience during the last few years.

But you are, I hope, going to take a temporary vow for two years. And a vow is an important thing: it is a contract you make direct with God. And I urge you, if you are going to ask permission to take a temporary vow for two years, that you fully understand that it *is* for two years. If you foresee that you are likely, after six months or a year, to change your mind, then please do not take temporary vows. If you are going into this two-year period looking, so to speak, over your shoulder, then please do not take a temporary vow: it is solemn and important and binds you for two years. And so, if you are going to ask to make your Profession, my advice to you is to take vows for the whole period of two years; then you enter upon that period with enthusiasm and determination, committing yourself to live for God in this manner of life for that period of time.

That would be right at any level, because it is only by entering into the life enthusiastically, positively, joyfully, that you will discover whether or not it is for you. Further, there is a sense of relief and release once you have committed yourself—when the debate going on in your mind ('Shall I, or shall I not?') is terminated. There is indeed nothing more liberating than the taking of solemn vows: the debate is closed, you are committed, there is no going back, the future is unknown, and you leave the vow to God. That is the attitude to have when you take solemn vows. Whatever your difficulties, it is a liberating thought. You are giving yourself to God and there is no going back. And that is the attitude you must have during the next two years if you take this temporary vow.

When you were postulants and we were discussing whether or not you should enter the monastery, I told you there were three questions you should put to yourself: Do I want to live with these persons? Do I want to do what they do? Do I see myself becoming the sort of person they are? These are three questions you might well put to yourselves again. Do you want to be one of us? Do you want to do what we do? Do you see yourself becoming the sort of persons we are? As to this third point: note how diverse we are, how different one from another. What I mean by this is, not that you should assume the mannerisms or attitudes of any particular person; you are to remain yourself, you as you are. But you do need to have a sort of instinct — the kind of reaction we have because we are monks, and not for any other reason.

No doubt during this last year you will have had some rude shocks about yourselves; if not, then your novitiate has been to some extent wasted. By now you will have learnt a good deal about yourself and will recognise, possibly in a way you did not earlier, that you have faults. In each one of you there is a fundamental flaw which can be your undoing — of that there is no question. A flaw of this nature can lead us to make fools of ourselves, to make some grave mistake. To recognise this flaw and learn to cope with it is one of the ways of remaining in the monastic life.

Now it does not matter if you have faults, provided two factors remain unshakable. First, you should be devoted to prayer. And this does not mean you are good at prayer or that you have a taste for prayer. It does mean, however, that you *want* to pray — not emotionally but in your will; that you know what you want to do and are determined to keep on; that sometimes — say within the last year — there has been a nostalgia for prayer, a real desire for prayer which, even though it can at times become faint, almost obliterated, does nevertheless prevent you from giving up. Secondly, you should genuinely want to belong to this Community: to throw in your lot with us, despite your faults and weaknesses. You should be ready to face an unknown future — in the company of these men on their way through life in search of God.

If you are critical of us, if you don't like us, if you feel we will rub you up the wrong way, then don't stay. We know we have our faults, that we are an imperfect community, but at least in our imperfections and weaknesses we stand together. And it is vital, if you join us, that you stand with us — sink with us if necessary. But you must want, in being professed, to be one of us. It is required of you that you be men of humility, men who recognise the value of obedience, not only because it conforms you to Christ but also because it leads you, helps you, in your search for the Father. You must be prepared to face difficulties manfully, bravely, cheerfully. We cannot have in the Community men with a 'chip on the shoulder'; we cannot have disillusioned men; we cannot have those who find everything wrong; we cannot have those who suppose that if all things were changed all would be better. No, you have to accept us as we are, and remember that in a monastery grumbling is a threat to unity and charity. This, let me say, does not preclude criticism that is positive: indeed you should work, as far as you can, to change what you think needs changing—but in a constructive manner. It is all a matter of attitude.

I emphasise this because we live in an age of protest, an age of questioning. Now much of this is good, but if it is to be an integral part of monastic life, then I for one think this life has no future. Today people coming into the monastery are bound to reflect the attitudes of the world; but we cannot allow the attitudes of the world to prevail in the monastery. In the old days, when we entered, we had attitudes which we had to leave behind. The same applies to you. That is what *conversio morum*[1] is about.

Remember too, that if you take vows, you remain the person you were before, with the temptations and the desires others have. It is almost certain—I would say certain—that you are going to find somebody in your lives with whom you could settle happily in the married state. There would be nothing surprising in that. But you have to face the fact, before you take vows, that there are going to be these trials and difficulties. Face them now, and if you are men of God and prayer—real monks—you will be able to cope.

As a novitiate you have been slow to learn a number of things. You have, I think, a good understanding of the theory of monasticism—a far better one, if I may say so, than the novitiate to which I belonged. You have asked yourselves some pretty profound questions: that is all to the good, and for that you are to be congratulated. You have not, however, been equally good at acquiring the monastic instincts. You have been, I think, slow in getting to the point. It is one thing to know the point, another to see it, another to live it. The Novice Master tells me that he thinks in your general training you are probably several months behind most novitiates. That is a bit sad; so you are going to have to put a spurt on. As you are men of ability and goodwill you should be able to do that. You have time to catch up: I urge you to do so.

27. 6. 70

Self-fulfilment

You have come here, as you are well aware, to seek God. Each person has to discover, in so far as he can, what is his way. That is the key: the will of God for each of us. You came here because you thought, and others whom you consulted agreed, that God was calling you to the monastic way of life. At the moment, as far as we can tell — and no doubt as far as you can see — this is what God wants you to do. As a Community we have welcomed you to live, pray, and work among us in this period which for you is probationary. We want you to be happy, contented. We want you to lead useful lives. We want you to attain self-fulfilment.

If, however, you are obsessed with self-fulfilment there is a good chance — that is putting it mildly — that you will not achieve it. Indeed, self-fulfilment is only achieved when the objects or targets we set ourselves are beyond our range. There is, of course, self-fulfilment of a bad kind and self-fulfilment that is good. The wrong kind, which is self-seeking, self-asserting, self-regarding, will lead you — and you don't need me to tell you — into very considerable misery in whatever walk of life you find yourself. St. Benedict is almost ruthless on this question of self-seeking — self-will. What he is aiming at is to eradicate from our lives — to save us from ourselves — those forms of self-seeking and assertiveness which lead us into misery and constitute a barrier between ourselves and God. There is nothing so subtle, so pervasive, as the enthronement of 'self' at the expense of others and of God.

That is the wrong kind of self-fulfilment. The right kind is expressed in the Gospel, in a paradox: the whole business of losing your life to save it. But that too can sound a bit negative. If you look in St. Paul you can find the inspiration contained in the Gospel message: that we should allow Christ to live in us;

that we should be receptive and responsive to the
promptings of the Spirit; that we should live as children
of God—address him as Abba, Father. A secret of
Christian living and therefore of the monastic life is
to see in each moment, each situation, each person, the
possibility of a meeting with Christ and, in Christ, with
the Father and the Holy Spirit.

Perhaps it helps if we distinguish between being
resigned to the will of God and surrendering to his
will. The word 'resigned' suggests putting up with
something, bearing it. 'Surrendering'—even though the
word has a connotation of weakness—has much more
the sense of acceptance, a voluntary acceptance, an
embracing of God's will, a going out to meet his will.

If we look at each moment as a point at which we
meet God and make it always a moment of love and
surrender to his will, then each moment of our lives
can and should become one in which we seek and find
God. That is what you came here for. And much of
the life here is organised to make this possible: to
provide opportunities to reflect, think, and become
increasingly aware of God's presence.

There is, we have said, a right kind of self-fulfilment
and a wrong one. We can deceive ourselves into
thinking that the wrong one is right. We can also, by
another trick of the mind, conceive the right one as
the wrong; so that when things are going well, when
life is smooth, when we have success, we can think that
this is something wrong. We meet from time to time
this strand of thinking in Christians; and so in this
matter a delicate balance has to be maintained in our
thinking and our acting. Let the words of our Lord
echo in your mind: to find your life you have to lose it,
so that you may live—no longer you but Christ within
you.

Do you find each other un-Christ-like? Let me put
it more harshly. Do you find that others madden you?
You have probably discovered that they do. Let me
put to you this sobering thought: if someone maddens
you, you may be sure you madden someone else! That
is a simple, straight, stark thought; but it is a help when
other people's idiosyncrasies make us lose our sense
of perspective. Yet we must get this right. Community
life is made up of a lot of small things. It is the small

courtesies that matter: small marks of consideration, thinking of each other, being sensitive to others, aware of their needs, aware of their moods, tactful in handling them, kind in rebuking them, gentle. In community life inevitably there are collisions. We should not accept this too lightly; we should always think them regrettable and do our best to remove things in us that cause irritation. We are not all equally sensitive to the needs of others. There is not a great deal we can do about that—except that if we are insensitive to others it is a good thing to discover the truth and try to adjust ourselves, train ourselves, to be sensitive.

I would like to talk about loneliness, particularly *Loneliness...* in the monastic life. It would unfortunately take too long.

There is, however, a right kind of loneliness and a wrong kind. More people in the world are lonely than are not. And often, small acts of consideration, small kindnesses—a mere nod of the head or a 'Good morning'—can make all the difference. There are some guests coming here. They will appreciate that kind of courtesy and consideration. And thrown together as you are in the confined atmosphere of the novitiate, you should practise this in your relations with one another. You did not decide together to join the Community; each of you made his decision singly. You have been thrown together by circumstances. Now, as Christians and as monks you must learn to live together.

7. 4. 71

On personal relationships

There are a great number of ways of relating to other people. We are bound to like some people more than others. In all our relationships we need to remember the important fact that each person is made to the image and likeness of God. Thus we ought to be able to see reflected in each something of God. Moreover each person is unique, and so he or she has something special to show which no one else has. That is the reason why each person whom I meet has a claim on my respect. It is also true that in some aspect each person is superior to me, because in my experience everybody I meet has qualities or capacities which I have not, or has them in greater measure. Even if this were not true, he would still have his own uniqueness which is his alone.

We can go further and reflect that in becoming man, God can be said to have become the image and likeness of man. To be absolutely accurate, I should point out that man, made to the image and likeness of God, does not become God in the way that God, becoming the image and likeness of man, did in fact become man. Perhaps we can see more clearly what I am trying to say if we think about seeing Christ in other people. What does this mean? It means, I suggest, that when a person is transformed by God's love, that person is made Christ-like.

This is important for all of us, whether married or not. It is a great help in understanding how the celibate should love. He should try to see the image and likeness of God in everybody: he must see Christ in all men. If the celibate is drawn to a particular person, then he will learn through his natural attraction how to do this (though he may have to struggle against being overwhelmed by the attraction); he may use the experience to seek Christ in all men and women. This approach will be applicable to everyone, but I am addressing myself to celibates.

We must not, then, be frightened of our capacity to love. If love is strong in us—and at times it will be—then we can use the experience to reflect on the great love God has for us and it can help us to discover the meaning of the words of St. John when he said 'God is Love'. There is the secret: try to discover the meaning of that and we can then discover the true meaning of celibacy. Human love leads to the discovery of the meaning of divine love; conscious of that love of God for us we shall then begin to love others in God. That discovery comes after much searching—and honest heart-searching in ourselves too. We are not able to survive as celibates unless we are faithful to prayer. It is in prayer that our experiences will become intelligible and manageable.

1976

Celibacy (i)

You are learning at the present time the art of community living. It is an art—and a delicate one—in which all kinds of excesses can be committed. No doubt you are already discovering from your own experience what you already knew—namely, the profound difference that can obtain between us; and this can give rise to obvious difficulties.

Each one of us is unique, absolutely unique, and behind that uniqueness is a purpose which ultimately is God's purpose; and that purpose of God is determined by his love. That is the total explanation of his creative and redemptive work; and so his love for each is different, but differentiated only by the object of the loving—which is ourselves, each one of us. As love emanates from God it cannot in itself change—increase or diminish. It is differentiated by us—to use simple terms—by the degree of our willingness to receive it.

The relationship between God and ourselves, between him and myself, is unique, and when you reflect that in him there is no change, no increase, no diminution, it follows that the totality of his love is concentrated on each one of us individually. A staggering, astounding thought. But you will find peace, happiness, tranquillity and freedom in your monastic life in proportion as this thought comes to dominate your mind and inspire your actions. And because what you have realised to be true in respect of yourself is equally true in respect of everyone else, it will guide and determine your attitude to others. In each individual there is a unique lovableness which no one else possesses, and which, therefore, in the eyes of God is infinitely precious—and I use these words deliberately. These are elementary, obvious reflections; but it is easy to be so preoccupied with a hundred and one things that we miss what is fundamental, and the reason behind it all.

The aspect of community life upon which I wish to *Emotions . . .* reflect at the present time is the understanding and handling—in our own life and in the guidance of others—of the affective part of ourselves: the emotional part, our affections. You must never be frightened of your affections. If you did not feel drawn to some

4

persons more than to others you would, I think, be a
very odd human being. That is the first thing—never
be frightened or surprised. Secondly, remember that
you cannot ignore your emotions, as if they did not
exist; you cannot live as if you had no affections.
Thirdly, these cannot be stifled: it is dangerous to try
to stifle them, to extinguish them, to live as if they were
not there. They are part of you.

To understand the rôle of one's affections in the
Christian life, in the monastic life, is not always easy.
It would be arrogant were I to claim to provide easy
—let alone infallible—solutions. I think, however, that
the art of coping with personal relations in which one's
emotions are involved is that of saying 'Yes' to others,
and very often 'No' to oneself. What does that mean?
It means we have to acquire a freedom in our relationship with others—an ease—but going with it must be
a control. In saying 'Yes' to others, I am making myself
available to them: I am not frightened of loving others
or of being loved by them. Often people are more
frightened of the latter than of the former. And by
control I mean a realisation of where the limits lie.
'Yes' to others spells freedom and ease; 'No' to oneself,
control. It is in this area that the key lies.

It is difficult to understand the rôle of celibacy in
the Christian life. The explanation given in modern
times that it is an 'eschatological dimension of the
Kingdom of God' is not particularly helpful to me
personally, though I can go along with it. To make a
particular kind of consecration of self to God we have
to be fully human. But can you be fully human in the
celibate state? That is the question which many ask,
and if you were to flip through the pages of some
psychologists you might well wonder. For myself, I
have not read a convincing explanation. My sole guiding light is Christ our Lord, whom I accept as being
both fully human and celibate. As so often, there is
in the life of Christ and in his teaching a paradox.
More than that, there is a sign of contradiction, so
that his teaching appears to contradict what to us
seems reasonable. If this were not so, I could not
accept the Cross—even followed by the Resurrection.
So much constitutes a stumbling-block—folly to the
Gentiles, but to us who believe . . . Theologians will

have to discover a way of presenting celibacy in the light of modern research and show us that we can be fully human and yet celibate. That we *can* be I accept in consequence, as I have said, of what I believe about Christ and, on an entirely different level, from what I have encountered in other persons, experientially. Celibacy is central to the monastic life.

The solution of our problems of emotion and affection and the problems which arise from our own sexuality is to acquire purity of heart in the true biblical and monastic sense. In our life we must practically and realistically seek the Lord and want him, with all that this means and entails. It is in this way that the problems are resolved and begin to fall into place: it is central to us in our life to seek him in purity of heart. That you will achieve, dear Brothers—all of us will achieve—only in so far as we come to understand the unique quality of God's love for each of us, and come to see the experience of love in our own lives as mirrors in which we can contemplate the divine love in respect of ourselves; to see in our own experience of love the way whereby we may achieve a response to that love which has first been given to us.

I would finally urge you to spend quite a lot of time looking at, mulling over, praying privately, the psalms. *Mulling over the psalms...* The more you look at them, the more you study them, the more you will see how they express in prayer the things I talk to you about. Perhaps you could spend some time looking at psalm 41, for instance; or better, psalm 62, and with these thoughts in mind turn them into prayer. Work hard to acquire a love of the psalms. Dear Brothers, persevere, persevere!

5. 7. 72

Celibacy (ii)

Celibacy affects us in what is most intimate and personal deep down in each one of us. It is something that we choose quite deliberately. Unfortunately, it is no more possible for the young monk to foresee how it is going to affect him later in life than it is possible for the young married man to know how his state of life is going to work out for him.

The problems of the celibate state change at different times in life. Earlier in life sexual and emotional problems are more in evidence; later it hurts at a deeper level (I am none too certain whether 'deeper' is the right word). It is, I suspect, the realisation of the need for the masculine 'I' to have the feminine 'Thou', certainly in terms of companionship, but more certainly in terms of the masculine 'I' wanting to possess and be possessed by the feminine 'Thou'('Possess' may sound too self-regarding, and a better phrase might be 'mutual self-giving'.

At the heart of celibacy there is always pain. It has to be so, because the celibate lacks something vital. But the pain is not to be grudged; the celibate forgoes the fulfilment of his sexual desires precisely because he recognises that his sexuality is a good thing. He renounces it because he knows that his Master did, and the Church from earliest times has instinctively known that other values can be gained as a result of that renunciation. God loves a cheerful giver.

Of course, we can romanticise about marriage; and we all know from our pastoral experience that marriage, like celibacy, is an art to be learned, with its own pitfalls and problems. It, too, has its renunciation.

Why then do we take on celibacy? I have never found it easy to give reasons. We talk about being more available to other people. That is true—or should be. We use the word 'witness'—we give witness through our celibacy to the eschatological dimension of the Kingdom of God. That is true, too, but I personally, I repeat, do not find that particularly helpful. Sometimes we just accept it as part of becoming a monk. That is singularly uninspiring.

For my part, two things are important: first, the fact that our Lord was celibate. Whatever reasons were important to him, I want to make mine. Our Lord was a virgin. That too is important. We should ponder on these truths in prayer. Secondly, from earliest times celibacy has been a value in the life of the Church (and indeed for many others too). It is a value that has been honoured and cherished all down the ages. It is in the tradition.

These two facts are reason enough for being celibate. Gradually, as life goes on, we see increasingly that it is a vocation. God calls some men and women to be celibates. If we are clear that we have been called to it, then we come, slowly perhaps, to glimpse the point.

The point—or one of them—is the capacity to grow in love towards God and man. That should be self-evident, but it is often forgotten. It is the point of any Christian life, married or not. But celibacy is a special way of loving. To realise this is a good starting point, for we have to avoid two extremes: the silliness of being seized by fear and the danger of misguided involvements with other people. A celibate must be a warm person and a good human being. Celibacy must make us more human, not less, more loving, and more lovable. But like all loving it must be controlled and disciplined. A celibate has to say 'Yes' to everyone with whom he comes into contact, and 'No' to himself in a hundred and one different kinds of situations. He is available to serve all with whom he comes into contact—he must give himself to all and not exclusively to one. And his service will be the more effective if it is accompanied by real controlled affection.

We should, too, never forget the respect that we must have for other people. It is not right, for example, to allow other people to fall in love with us. That is a far greater danger than our falling in love with others. If we are silly (and vanity is the danger here) we can cause pain and hurt; and that is wrong.

So we have to be good human beings, warm and spontaneous in our relationships with other people, but sane and sensible, recognising our frailty, remembering that we are men and retain our virility and the power to attract and be attracted. A strong interior life of prayer and a love of our monastic life will be our main safeguards in face of the dangers, and will provide the contact within which to work out how to consecrate our celibacy to God and to discover its secret and its value.

1976

A man of God

When you and I were talking before you entered the
novitiate I warned you that in your lifetime you might
easily find profound changes not only in the Church
but in the monastic life. I told you, too, that in this
Community you would find considerable differences of
opinion on many subjects. Without claiming to be a
prophet, I do indeed foresee changes in your lifetime,
if not in that of the rest of us.

Do understand that it is not given to any generation
—and certainly not to ours—to have the last word on
any issue that is being currently debated. We shall
never be able to say that the development of doctrine
concerning the Church, the priesthood, the Eucharist,
or obedience, has reached a point at which nothing
more can be said. And this is a profound truth, in the
sense that we are not meant to live solely by intellectual
convictions; we are meant more and more to open
ourselves to the Spirit. Discerning the Spirit and the
guidance of the Spirit is extremely difficult. But do not
be upset or worried if the Community you think of
joining is not able to give a quick, easy, convincing
definition of, say, a priest, or even a monk. In the
ultimate analysis there is something more important.

I would also like to make the point that in our time
we are being called in a special way by God to achieve
a radical detachment—in the sense that we are asked
to change long-established practices; and this can be
a painful process. What is still more painful is having
to modify or change our thinking. That is extremely
painful; and many of us in these last few years have
suffered more pain, more agony, than we have revealed.
But we have had to try and see this in the presence of
God—to ask what he is trying to give us or show us.
For my part, I can only understand it as a call from
him to a detachment at a level we have not experienced
hitherto.

A thought came to me this morning as I was listening
to the homily. We were told to pray that God's will be
done in us and through us. That is the really important
thing: to be open to God that his will may be done in
us—his will, in his way, not his will in our way. The
openness we must have if we are to fulfil his purpose

in and through us, as individuals and as a Community, is a fundamental monastic attitude. But we cannot live without convictions, and many of our past convictions may prove to be assumptions. One thing, however, is certain and unchangeable, namely, that it is incumbent on each one of us in the monastic life to become—the phrase, I think, is self-explanatory—a man of God. That is what matters: to be single-minded, whole-hearted in our determination to respond to whatever God asks of us.

Now in the monastic life there are certain facets which permit of no wavering. I shall mention three only.

Obedience. I cannot tell you what the theology of obedience is; I am incapable of resolving problems concerning it which have been thrown up in recent years. But two things I know. Experientially I have discovered the power of obedience in a monk to whom it is an important value; and what I understand I have learnt, paradoxically, from monks whom, in one situation or another, I have been called upon to command. To my way of thinking, therefore, it would be senseless to devalue or diminish the importance of obedience in the monastic life. I would go further. I would say that if a monk has not this value at heart—whatever may be going on in his head—he is falling short of his vocation and harming not only himself but the Community; and it is only too easy to whittle away the importance of obedience. Moreover, I have observed the paradox of obedience. It suggests constraint—the reverse of freedom; whereas in fact it is the path to an interior freedom: a total availability to God. I have discovered, too, that in a monk the desire to obey, when this matures, is in fact the outcome of a freedom achieved.

Prayer. Prayer in community and private prayer. Prayer is not only something which enables me to be more effective in my ministry. It is not only a means of attaining personal fulfilment. Prayer is practised for its own sake. It is its own purpose. A monastic life is a poor one if prayer does not have the primacy in the mind of the monk. In whatever circumstances a monk finds himself; whatever the calls of school-work or his parish (these are necessary: even, at times, imperative), if these demands diminish the primacy in his life of prayer, to that extent his monastic vocation is defective. There can be no compromise here.

Poverty is a difficult subject. It is a matter of simplicity and frugality; but most of all a sense of dependence — dependence on God, dependence on the Community. Dependence is a fact in the life of everyone. But as monks we live that dependence consciously, as an act of recognition that ultimately all things come from God. This is where the rôle of permission comes in. When I ask permission, this is an outward recognition that God is the source of all things. It is also a recognition that I do not own the object in question: I use it by permission of the Community. In a sense, when I ask the Prior's permission, I am asking that of the Community. I am recognising my dependence on God. It would, I think, be a pity to let these practices drop out of our lives without appreciating their value.

Do not judge the Community on superficialities. It is a strong Community: a group of men dedicated to the service of God. We have not all attained an equal perfection. It is not for you to judge: leave that to God. And if you persevere you will find, as St. Benedict promises, peace at a depth beyond, I suspect, your comprehension. To discover it, it is worth hanging on.

5. 4. 72

'Yes' to God

There are four criteria whereby St. Benedict asks the authorities to judge whether you are suitable for the monastic life. Are you truly seeking God? Are you zealous for the work of God? Are you prepared to embrace a life in which obedience plays an important part; and are you prepared to accept humiliations? — the word is *opprobria* in the Latin. The word 'humiliations' is a mistranslation; I take it to mean contradictions — those things which stand in the way, those things which put us 'out of sorts', those things which come to depress, and the rest. There comes a crucial moment in the life of a novice and a young monk when he ceases to think of his monastic life as something which is there for him to attain through self-fulfilment, or realisation, or even his own personal happiness. He moves from that position to recognising it as a response to a 'call': a call made in which he answers: 'Yes, I answer that call'. This involves a considerable difference of attitude of mind.

I say that there is a moment in the life of a novice and young monk when he has got to see it in this way; but it is also true to say that the rest of us have constantly to re-learn this simple fact: we come here in response to a call that has been made to us by God, to follow Christ in the monastic way. Gradually over the years we come to see perhaps more clearly those sayings of the Gospel: 'You only find your life if you lose it'; 'the seed has to die before it can grow', etc. Again, that contains lessons for us to go on learning all over again.

Your novitiate life is unexciting, uneventful. Perhaps it is also bleak for considerable periods of time. I want to emphasise just one point. What you have to learn is that each act of yours has to become an act of love: your response in love to a love which has first been given to you. This is a very important thing to learn, because later on in your monastic life you will, and should, find satisfaction in the work that you do or in the interests which you pursue. Thus you can find happiness, fulfilment, self-realisation and the rest. But for us, as monks, that is not enough; these have to be acts of love. They must be acts of love for every Christian, but in a special way, perhaps more consciously, for monks. That has to go, *pari passu*, with an evolution in your prayer life; but I shall come to that in a moment. Do not, of course, think that your monastic life is going to be all enjoyment and self-fulfilment; we all have to face monotony, to face doing things we would rather not do. We all tend to think that the grass is greener on the other side of the fence; we all run into our frustrations – the *opprobria* are part of our living. It is important to remember that carrying on under those circumstances is not necessarily more meritorious than when you are throwing yourself into things which you enjoy. The basis of merit is not hardship: the basis of merit is love. True, monotony and difficulty can certainly be a proof of love. When you really love, nothing is too menial, nothing is too monotonous, nothing too trivial.

It is really important how you think about the love of

God the Father, the Son, and the Holy Spirit; and how
to pray. Think daily about God's great love for you.
There is nothing more revealing of his love for us than

No greater the fact that God the Son became man, and died on the
love . . . Cross: 'No greater love has a man than to lay down his
life for his friends.' That is one of the most wonderful
things that was ever said. It is one thing to say something, another to do it. In the crucifix you see, in the
most vivid, convincing way, God speaking to us about
his great love. Think, too, of your own need for love,
your own capacity to love; that too will enable you to
have a glimpse of what God's love must be. That
should be a constant theme in your meditation, in
your prayer.

If we really were good Christians and good monks,
we would show a zest, a joy in everything we did,
because our motive would be an act of love for the
beloved. It is true, too, that doing things to please
another enables us in some way to know that other
person. And this is true of our relationships with God.
Doing things especially to please him is one of the ways
whereby we get to know him and, as has been said by
that medieval writer, William of St. Thierry, 'You have
to love God and through that love come to a knowledge
of him'. Do not forget, too, how important are your
relationships with your fellow novices, and with the
brethren as a whole. They have to be very much related
to your love of God, and your search for God. Take
as a motto, or as axiomatic, that a monk should be
pleasing to other people, and pleasant. It is important
to realise that as a member of a monastic community
you are responsible for the happiness and cheerfulness
of everyone else in the Community. Anybody making
that statement feels hypocritical: it is a difficult ideal
to live up to. Nevertheless, it is an important ideal,
because in our practice of it we are showing, or acquiring—both at the same time—our love of God. In each
of the brethren we have to see the face of Christ, and
this means that we will seek to find Christ, seek to
please Christ, in the other—which means treating
people with enormous respect as well as with delicacy.
You yourself must be cheerful.

24. 4. 75

3. Simple Profession

Put on the mind of Christ

In the course of this evening I have been puzzling what to say to you: what would be valuable, what would be helpful. Then it occurred to me that it is not what is said by me that really matters, but what the Holy Spirit reveals to you in your heart.

If you think of the three vows normally taken in religious life—obedience, poverty, and celibacy—a number of points come to mind. Whatever be the interpretation of these in modern theology, however they are lived in practice in this Order or that, I would commend you to reflect on what lies at the heart of each.

To take the vow of obedience is primarily to consecrate one's freedom to God. It is to recognise the pre-existing fact that in human life freedom is limited by the demands made upon us by God: he is the author of our freedom, the object of this freedom, the master of this freedom. In making your profession you are acknowledging his omnipotence, his total claim on you.

By professing poverty you are acknowledging that God is our treasure; that, as human beings, if we do not in some way possess him, we are poor, very poor—deprived.

By your vow of celibacy you acknowledge that God is the object of all our desires; that he is the ultimate love which alone can satisfy the restless heart of man. The tragedy in our religious life is that we can and do cheat. We cheat by forgetting that we have publicly professed to make God's will our own. We cheat when we make other things our ultimate pleasure and forget what we professed. And we can cheat in our vow of celibacy when we seek or condone in ourselves an illicit sensual satisfaction.

If we are to put on the mind of Christ, we who are already incorporated into him by our baptism, we are *The mind of Christ . . .* by our Profession deliberately conforming our lives to his. We want to be obedient as he was obedient to his Father's will; we want to be poor because he was poor; we want to be celibate because he was celibate. In our intimacy with our Lord in our life of prayer we shall come to see in his obedience, in his poverty, in his

celibacy, something of the secret which motivated him
and ought, as life goes on, to become our secret.

Ours it is to put on the mind of Christ, because it is
in our relationship to him and with him and through
him that we go to the Father. Life in our monastic
setting is a search for God—with and in Christ—for
the Father. It is a pilgrim way. But in joining this
Community you do not stand alone. By your vow of
stability you root yourself in the Community and move
forward with it. You have to be prepared for change.
You must not allow yourself to become static in your
thinking, or in the stage of prayer you have reached,
or in your outlook. You have to change because in
doing so you prepare for the end of the journey.

The end of the journey. This leads me to say a word
about hope, trust, and confidence in God. Many of
our problems derive from the fact that we do not trust
God; that we allow ourselves to be thrown back on
self, to depend on self, to look for our salvation within
our own resources—our thinking, ability, talents. That
constant trust of which Julian of Norwich speaks, that
'all will be well and all manner of thing will be well',
should be our aim. It is difficult. We must live in the
present, with the task which is ours today, with the
people with whom our lot is cast. We must live in this
world renewed and refashioned by Christ by reason of
the Incarnation. We must look forward to the future,
when all will be peace, serenity, happiness.

Perhaps in our contemporary spirituality we think
too little of the joy of heaven, the happiness of heaven.
It is good to look forward with expectation, with
excitement, to the moment when we shall be dissolved
and be with Christ,[1] be with Christ in the Father. This
is the kind of grace for which we ought to be praying,
the expectation with which we should look forward,
thus putting into perspective—God's perspective—the
things of the world: our problems, our desires, our lives.

24. 1. 74

A continual search

Things are by no means straightforward in the monas-

[1] Phil. 1:23.

tic life today. There are, as you know, differences of
opinion on many subjects: the kind of work we should
do; the type of school we should run; how the school
should be organised; the values it should inculcate; our
life of prayer; ways of celebrating the Eucharist; the
manner of reciting Office in choir. There are differences
of opinion concerning the very principles of the spiritual
life. These differences of opinion are realities and will,
to some degree, provide the background against which
you will be making your Profession. Moreover, these
differences have to be dealt with constructively, with
charity, good sense, and good humour. There must be
mutual tolerance, patience, and, above all, a continual
search for God's will, which is more important than the
realisation of one's own monastic dreams. We need to
remind ourselves that the forces destructive of community life and community happiness operate more
quickly and effectively than those which construct and
build up the house of God.

Such then is the context within which you will be
taking your vows. You do not take them in a vacuum.
You are joining a particular group of men engaged
for the present in specific activities, with all the good and
bad that you get in any body of men who are inevitably
imperfect.

Your vow of stability roots you in this Community
and loyalty to it and your fellow monks: you should
do nothing to wound, hurt, or arouse suspicion. In
living out the highest observance of your vow of
stability you are not debarred from criticism, but your
criticism must always be constructive, sympathetic, and
never corrosive.

Love your vows. Treasure them, live them and do
not shirk the demands they will make upon you.
Externally, to the untrained eye, the demands may not
seem considerable; but within, in our minds and hearts,
they will be great. These demands will reach the point
at which our own judgment on how things should be
will strain even the integrity of our thinking and put
pressure on our personal happiness. You cannot take
vows and live in a monastic community without being
called upon daily to make sacrifices. If you do not feel
equal to that, then I beg you not to proceed.

Obedience is the test of our total availability to God:

the measure of our love of him. I urge you not to be
selective in your obedience, interpreting the rules or the
mind of the Superior in ways favourable to your personal manner of thinking. If you only obey when a
demand seems reasonable or fits into your philosophy
of life, that way, I warn you, lies spiritual disaster and
unhappiness. You may consider that our vows are
personal, in that they are a personal commitment of
ourselves to God, but the Community has a corporate
life and the vows a communal aspect.

Let me illustrate this from the vow of what is called
'conversion of manners': *conversio morum*. Each one
of us is called by that vow to work at his personal
sanctification—a change of heart, a change in our way
of behaving, a purifying of intentions. But the Community collectively must work for the same end.

Think clearly, as men of God should, about the
Community you are joining. Try to see the value of what
we are and what we do. Take it that there is a great deal
in the monastic life, as led here, which is pleasing to
God—many monks who are prayerful, hard-working,
with high ideals, labouring obscurely, thoughtfully, and
without complaining. Be of that number. You will find
happiness and receive the blessing of God if you are
unflagging in search of him and in doing his will. It is
not a soft life: indeed such a life would be unworthy
of us as human beings, apart from our vocation to
follow Christ. The peace it brings is hard-won and,
believe me, brings suffering. And yet it is a peace
unruffled by the tempests assailing us on this side and
that. It is the peace of knowing that whatever are our
personal deficiencies, whatever our limitations, there
is a God, nevertheless, who wants us and loves us—
each one of us.

16. 1. 75

4. Solemn Profession

Love is reckless

This week I have participated in three historical events
within our congregation: the consecration of a Benedic-

tine bishop[1] and the election of two abbots. Yet none of them has given me greater joy than will your Profession tomorrow.

You are answering God's call to follow him: 'Go, sell all you have and follow me.' During the days after your Profession,[2] when you will be totally alone with God, you will be able to meditate on the step you have taken: a step, dear Brothers, which is final, irrevocable. And that is not a daunting or depressing thought; on the contrary, it is exhilarating. No three days of your lives will bring you such happiness. And the gift you are making is final. You do not know what the future has in store for you. You do not know what difficulties lie ahead. You do not know by what tortuous ways God will lead you. All you know is that you have given yourselves to God; and this will bring joy, peace, and blessing, for God is never outdone in generosity. But if in your giving there is any taking back; if there are second thoughts, I warn you, your sorrow will be great.

You are responding to the invitation; 'Follow me.' *Follow me ...* 'But how?' you ask. God has told you, through the circumstances of your life, the events that brought you here, the years you have spent with us. He says: 'Go to this Community and learn my ways. You will learn from the experience of others who have gone before you. Go to this *dominici schola servitii*, this school of the Lord's service. You will learn from the collective experience of monks who have been through this house.'

You have come here to learn the ways of God, through the experience of others to which you will adjust your own. But you do not come here, dear Brothers, just to take, just to receive. You come also to give. A monastery is not static: it is moving with the times. You are aware how this Community has changed since the foundation at Dieulouard in 1608.[3] And yet, despite change, certain characteristics have emerged that are an expression of our life here. These are not

[1] The Right Rev. B. C. Butler, O.S.B.
[2] The newly Solemnly Professed monk does not speak for three days — a symbol of his being re-born in Christ, from death to life, Crucifixion to Resurrection.
[3] In 1608 the English Benedictine Congregation of pre-Reformation days was linked to the post-Reformation Congregation by the Profession of three monks (of Ampleforth—Dieulouard) by Fr. Sigebert Buckley, the last surviving monk of Westminster Abbey.

exclusively ours: they are found in good measure elsewhere. But they *are* our characteristics, thank God,
and we are proud of them; and you must be proud of
them too.

What are these characteristics? I will underline four
of them.

First, a conviction in the minds of all the monks
here—even though we do not always live up to this—
that 'first things come first'. As I hope you have discovered, the monks in our Community try to love God
to the best of their ability. There is a love of the Mass.
There is a love of the Office—not that they always
understand the Office; not that there are not times when
it is burdensome; but they realise that when they are in
choir, that is where they want to be, and they know that
if obedience calls them out of the choir, this is not a
release, it is a deprivation.

Secondly, charity. In this Community charity is real.
Forgiveness comes readily. We are tolerant of one
another's foibles, stupidities, weaknesses. Yes, we are
mutually generous. There is charity, I repeat, in this
Community. And when there is charity, God is there.

Thirdly, hard work. Our service of God involves us
in the school; in caring, too, for the faithful in indus-
trial towns. It is a whole-hearted service, bringing with
it self-denial. By working hard we earn our living; and
because our work is creative we are sharing in God's
creativity. We are creating. We are building. We are
building the image of Christ in the boys. We are bringing Christ to the pagan areas we serve. We recognise,
too, that of all the ascetical activities of which spiritual
writers speak, there is no substitute for work.

Fourthly, loyalty. Sometimes it is misunderstood by
outsiders as a kind of smugness. Perhaps we give that
impression. But it is not smugness; it is what a monk
from another monastery, speaking of our Community,
called *pietas*—*pietas* in the right sense: *pietas* in relation
to God, *pietas* in relation to each other. A loyalty
which leads us to support each other in difficulties, to
help each other in our weaknesses, a loyalty which
derives from charity.

These four qualities we look forward to finding in you.
Indeed we would not have accepted you for Profession
if we thought they were lacking. But they have to become

stronger and deeper. And they will do so if you live your vows, if your life becomes a *conversio morum*, if you have true insight into stability—which means this acceptance of the Community in its totality: its work, its strength, its weakness, the things you like and those you dislike. Dear Brothers, you make your Profession tomorrow. You accept us as we are, you love us as we are.

And then obedience. You give yourselves to God: 'Go, sell what you have.' You give your riches to the poor and yourselves to God; you have nothing you can call your own, not even, in a sense, yourselves. You lay yourselves symbolically on the altar when your vows are put there at the Offertory. That is you. Your gifts. Everything God has given you. And the Church, who accepts this gift of yourselves in the name of God, will direct you in the name of God. 'He who hears you, hears me.' You give yourself to God, in and with Christ. You conform to the obedience of Christ, who became obedient even to death on the Cross; for which reason he has been raised up and given a name above all other names.

Make your gift whole-heartedly. Make it recklessly. Love is reckless.

22. 12. 66

Through thick and thin

It is a joy to us when a young man decides to give *Words of* himself to God in this Community. Inevitably, now *welcome ...* that you have been here for some years, we know you, with your strong points and your frailties, and on your side you can presume that we have come to enjoy your company and to value you. We hope, too, and expect that your Solemn Profession will give you deep joy, not only because you are consecrating yourselves to God, but because you are looking forward, we hope, to living, praying, and working with us.

The one thing of which we can always be proud is *A cause for* being a monk. As far as we are concerned, in saying *pride ...* that we say everything. We have no boast other than that we are monks. And a monk is a Christian who is called by God to live out the logic of his baptismal

5

vows in a particular way. The Christian life demands for most people, especially as we approach maturity, some kind of consecration. For some it is the married state. For us it is the monastic way of life, in which we determine to seek God in a special manner—to strive constantly for union with God. We have no other source of pride: we want to be known as nothing other than monks.

Till death us do part . . .   When you have taken your vows, throw in your lot with us, with no reservations. Stick to us through thick and thin. If, tomorrow, you were to stand at the altar not taking monastic vows but publicly declaring your love to your betrothed, making your marriage vows, you would promise to be true to her, for richer for poorer, in sickness and in health, 'till death us do part'. Is the vow which you are going to take here tomorrow any less than this? No, it is the same. You have dedicated yourself to us, sharing our strength, weakness, failures. For better or for worse.

The rubrics demand that we put before you the difficulties in the monastic life. You are aware how many these are, and no doubt you will find more. But do not let these dominate your thoughts. Be dominated by the thought that God's love has chosen you. You cannot have mathematical or physical certainty that God has called you; that you are suited to the monastic way of life—you can never have that sort of certainty. But you can be morally certain that we in the Community have for our part decided that you are called by God, that you are suited to what is required of you. And you have declared that you want this. Never doubt that God has called you. If you feel tempted to doubt, presume—and presume rightly—that the devil is at work.

Make your gift whole-heartedly, prepared for any eventuality, any possibility. You will find obedience a trial. Curiously, it is often not what you are told to do that hurts, but being removed from things which you like doing. Often a monk can accept before God in his prayers to be removed from a task he is doing; but sometimes it is very difficult to accept this psychologically. It is possible to accept it in his prayers, yet remain 'put out'. One has, I think, to learn, while still young, how to be torn from tasks one likes without being 'put out'. I recall a monk here who gave himself to whatever he was doing, so enthusiastically, so whole-heartedly, that one might have thought that this was his whole life. Yet inwardly he was detached. When asked to relinquish the tasks he had done for a long time he accepted this with an extraordinary simplicity and ease. In that moment the true worth of this monk was revealed: he had accepted under obedience the circumstances determined by his Superiors, and they had sanctified him.

3. 9. 68

Be obedient to one another

The monastic life is an unrelenting, keen, joyful search for God. Neither the work we do nor the Community shared with our brethren has primacy in our lives. Our primacy is to seek the face of God in all circumstances, in all persons. It is a pity—more, it is a tragedy—if a monk loses the desire to pray, loses his nostalgia for God. However busy you may be, however distracted, however complex life may become, you must not lose the desire to pray. The desire to pray is one thing, the obligation another, and they are not necessarily incompatible. I make the distinction only because there are times in our lives when it is not easy to pray; when we think we have lost the desire to pray. Hence the importance of recognising the obligation imposed upon us, which enables us, in our frailty and weakness, to persevere. In the life of prayer, fidelity and persistence in the face of all odds, all difficulties, are paramount. These enable us to find again the desire for prayer which, so it seemed, we had lost. *The desire for prayer . . .*

In embracing the monastic life we embrace a set of values different from those generally prevalent in the world. Striving for success, getting to the top, cutting a fine figure—we turn our backs on all this. *Frugality simplicity . . .*

To embrace celibacy is an astonishing thing, and indeed, difficult. Yet your experience will teach you why in the tradition of the Church it has been a constant value. It is difficult to control the emotions, the affective side of our lives. Let me say just this: all that is most deeply human in us must be touched and guided by that Spirit to whom is appropriated the word Love. *Fully human . . .*

We must be human, and fully human, with all the warmth and affection which belongs to the fully human. But you will already have understood that to be fully human, in the sense in which I am speaking, presupposes a control, sometimes an abnegation, not always easy to exercise. But control and deep human warmth are not necessarily inconsistent.

An aspect of obedience... In everyday life we encounter all kinds of situations which are a constraint upon our initiative and our freedom in carrying out our tasks. Other people's plans, other people's arrangements, other people's ideas or, quite simply, other people, frustrate us in one way or another. We are prevented from pursuing our ends, from carrying out our ideas as we would wish, because there are others who have plans and ideas—or simply because there are others! This, I think, is what St. Benedict had in mind when he talked about being obedient to each other. He did not mean just taking orders from others: he meant, rather, accepting the limitations which others impose upon us by the very fact that they are 'others'.

A humble heart... The great Benedictine quality: humility. There can be no true love of God, no true love of our neighbour, except it come from a humble heart. And it is very, very difficult to be humble. It comes not so much from within as from outside. We will find situations, circumstances and persons who will impose upon us the necessity to become humble—a quality difficult to attain and yet basic, for it entails emptying ourselves to be filled with the spirit of Christ. Read what St. Benedict says and translate it into contemporary ways of thinking.

11. 9. 73

'. . . *a bold step, a different logic* . . .'

The process whereby we come to a decision concerning a monastic vocation may seem cumbersome: the whole thing from the initial visits and interviews to this present moment, the eve of the Solemn Profession. We are not infallible—that goes without saying. But there is in this Community much experience and wisdom and good sense; the brethren are at their best when consulted on matters of grave importance. The step you are taking is indeed of grave importance, and you are allowed to take it because we think it is the right one for you. Where does the hand of God come into this? We need faith to recognise God's action in matters of such a kind. You must have faith, not in human wisdom or argument, but in the fact that God speaks in this way— through circumstances. God may even guide a man to a right decision for a wrong reason! The convergence of opinion within the Community concerning you is an important fact which neither you nor I can lightly disregard.

God speaks, too, within you—through your inclinations, desires, thoughts. The voice is not always clear and compelling. Sometimes it appears muffled. It is not always easy to interpret doubts and fears—they can come from deep within us or far back in the story of our lives. Guidance from another can be our only salvation. Paul was struck blind after his initial vision; Thomas too had doubts. In the end it must be a bold step: for some, into darkness, for all of us, into the unknown—a bold step: resolute, courageous, with no looking back.

Tomorrow, when you make your Profession, do not see it as the closing of a debate within yourself and with others, but as your answer to God's call. Your future will no longer be in your hands; it will be made known to you through the different acts of obedience that will be required of you. Yours is not a 'career' in the sense normally given to that word; your *conversio morum* implies a different logic, based on other premises —the following of Christ along the monastic way. And you become one of us, one of this family, for always. And this is the point at which to say to you in a special way: 'Welcome!' What you will do tomorrow will be pleasing to God. It is also greatly pleasing to us.

20. 12. 75

5. Ordination

Tu es sacerdos in aeternum

Within a few days of the Ordination it may seem odd

to begin a talk on the priesthood by referring to the present crisis among the clergy. But a crisis is a moment of change. And without doubt, whatever rôle the priesthood will ultimately assume in the Church, this will be under the guidance of the Holy Spirit. You will know that this is to be a major item on the agenda of the Synod of Bishops next October. A working paper has been circularised among the Bishops' Conferences entitled *De sacerdotio ministeriali*, to be discussed at different levels in the Church. It is a working paper, not a 'schema', not even a draft of a schema. It has, of course, been much criticised.

The debate concerns the priest in search of his identity. Now we all recognise that the rôle of the priest in the Church has changed and is changing. There is a general recognition, too, that the social status of the priest is different from that of yesterday. Moreover the problem of celibacy is acute. It has been said: 'Doubtless there is unbelief among a number of priests, but among the vast majority of those who find themselves in a state of crisis, the kernel of their faith remains unaffected. But they can no longer summon up "faith" in historically-bound dogmatic formulae, moral principles and ecclesiastical regulations.' There does indeed exist a malaise among priests throughout the world. Furthermore, study of the Scriptures and historical research have, perhaps, re-orientated the minds of people on the origins of the priesthood.

There are two major documents of the Second Vatican Council which have to be understood, it seems to me, before one can develop a proper theology of the priesthood today. These are *Lumen gentium* on the Church, and *Gaudium et spes* on the rôle of the Church in the modern world: these are key documents of the Vatican Council. And it is axiomatic that one cannot understand the theology of the priesthood except in relation to the attitude of the Church to the world. To be brief, *Lumen gentium* underlines the Church as the People of God assembled to hear and to respond to the Word of God, Jesus Christ, who liberates and reconciles all men through the outpouring of the Spirit. In that context the priest is seen, not so much as an official acting on behalf of a system but, as has been well said, as a witness of hope. *Gaudium et spes* provides a fresh and positive attitude towards the world: towards science, technology, politics, war—to the concerns and the needs of all human beings. And seen against the background of the teaching of *Gaudium et spes*, the priest cannot consider himself as outside the world, as having rejected its values or as having turned his back on it. He is to be seen much more as a prophet who gives meaning to God's creation and sings its praises. It is against the background of *Gaudium et spes* that the rôle of the priesthood will be understood and developed. The idea, for instance, of part-time professional work and political involvement are actual questions of today.

It is not for me to assess the importance of these different approaches to the priesthood: they are still the subject of debate and call for further reflection. But if one may hazard a guess, priests will increasingly be ordained from the ranks of the laity—particularly men who, in a world in which there will be increased leisure, will retire at an earlier age. This will be important, because we shall come to see that the priesthood is not to be regarded as a caste apart, but as having a function within the entire People of God.

Our situation as Benedictines is somewhat different, *Monk-priests ...* because we are monk-priests. Let it be said, as on previous occasions, that the monastic vocation is one thing, the vocation to the priesthood another. But priests, in the foreseeable future at any rate, will continue to come from the People of God, whether lay or religious. In our particular case, this combination of priest and monk is something which we have inherited from our past and it will not necessarily prevail in the future; but in our present circumstances it is indispensable. Does the combination of priest and monk blur the clarity of each of the vocations? I would emphasise that the monastic vocation does give a special character to the priesthood as exercised by monks, and *vice versa*. We shall never be able to predicate of the monk-priest all that we can predicate of the priest in general, because we cannot, in being ordained and in exercising our priesthood, cease from being monks.

The question which is much discussed today is the priesthood of the faithful. Are we not all baptised priests? We know this is so, in the sense that there is

only one priesthood of Christ, and within that priesthood a diversity of function. The ministerial priesthood
is to be distinguished from the priesthood of the faithful
(sometimes called the 'general priesthood of the faithful'). A sentence from *Presbyterorum ordinis* (the decree
on the priesthood in the Second Vatican Council) is,
I think, illuminating: 'Through this ministry (it is
referring to the ministerial priesthood) the priesthood
of Christ touches the ecclesial body, and the common
priesthood of the faithful is brought to the full exercise
of its office.' What it says is that it is the rôle of the
ministerial priesthood to bring to its full exercise—and
to its full expression—the priesthood of the entire body
of Christ. And so at the altar the priest is present to
give effect to, to express, the priesthood of the People
of God there assembled. We must always, I think, go
back to the fundamental fact of the one priesthood
which is the priesthood of Christ, in which we all share
in different degrees; and for those who are consecrated
to the ministerial priesthood of the Church there is a
difference of kind.

The question, too, is sometimes asked today whether
the priest is the delegate of the community or is he the
representative of Christ? He is, from one point of view,
the delegate of the community, in so far as he is drawn
from the community, is one of the community—is
presented, indeed, by the community to the Bishop for
ordination. On the other hand, he is Christ's representative, in so far as he is consecrated especially to be, when
he functions at the altar, the ikon of Christ: Christ the
head of each community when assembled, and the
presence of Christ manifested through this sign of
which the priest is a part. This is the doctrine of
Presbyterorum ordinis, when it says: 'Every priest in his
own way represents the person of Christ himself.' Hence
the solemnity of the occasion which we shall be celebrating on Sunday: the solemn consecration of four of
our Community to this task, this great function, in the
Church, which is the priesthood—the ministerial
priesthood.

*Ikon of
Christ . . .*

It is difficult to convey what it means to say, for the
first time, the words of consecration and to realise that
it is the first person singular which we are using. I know
little of the theology of the priesthood but something

of the current debates. There is an experience which transcends the theologising in one's mind and is much greater than the debate which must go on in the Church concerning these matters. It is the stark realisation that I am using the first person singular; that it is my voice, my hands, my mind, that are engaged in this tremendous act which is central to the Eucharist, in which Christ is manifested through my person. At this moment, which surpasses all others, I am the ikon of Christ, the image of Christ. I am being used by Christ so as to associate myself with all that he was doing at the Last Supper, on Calvary, in his redemptive act. Moreover, as I preside at this Eucharistic assembly, I draw others who are present into the work of Christ.

There are other words in the *Presbyterorum ordinis* which strike me: 'The consecration received is not a passive sign, but rather a dynamic force directing the whole life of the priest in the service of God and man and so pervading all of his person.' I am, at my ordination, the recipient of a 'dynamic force', and one cannot but ask why this force has been so little in evidence. Every priest must surely be conscious of the short-comings in himself. I sometimes wonder whether it is not because in the exercise of the priesthood one makes the mistake of depending too much on one's own expertise, one's own skill and gifts, and insufficiently on the realisation that the consecrating of the priest, the ordination of the priest, is a communication of the Holy Spirit; and that one is not sufficiently confident in the power of this same Spirit, not sufficiently trustful of him, not sufficiently in touch with the Spirit. It is true that in talking as I am now, I am not making the distinction some of us have been brought up to make between the actions of the priest *ex opere operato* and his actions *ex opere operantis*. Whether that distinction is either helpful or valid today is not for me to say. But I am asking why it is that we who have been given such tremendous powers seem to make little use of them? The answer can be given in part: none of us can measure the good he does, and from most of us the good we do is hidden. So often we fail to see the good we ourselves do but, thank God, we often see the good done by others. So collectively, can it not be said that the priesthood—or priests in

general – does not give, does not contribute, in proportion to the gifts bestowed on the day of ordination?
I simply ask the question and leave it at that.

In the spiritual life there will be for all of us an
experience of one kind or another, not realised perhaps
at the time but in retrospect, that something has happened to us: perhaps an understanding has been granted,
a conviction implanted or a change of direction revealed
which we see later as having been the work of God, the
work of the Spirit.

The moment of ordination is for the ordinand a
moment of transformation; and one of the joys of
that day is the realisation that, whereas everything
else can be taken from you, even your reason, no one
can take away your priesthood: *Tu es sacerdos in
aeternum*. The tragedy of leaving the priesthood strikes
one most on reflecting that if you renounce living as a
priest, you cannot renounce your priesthood. You are
a priest *in aeternum*. You realise on ordination day
that you have been given a tremendous power – one
which cannot be taken from you. On ordination day
there is the joy of the Mass – looking forward to saying
Mass. For a time this is vivid; then perhaps, as the
years roll by, it becomes less vivid. What I am trying
to put across is that there are and must be in our service
of God moments of light, moments of warmth. These
normally do not last, but we have the consolation of
living in their after-glow.

Our prayer on Sunday for those to be ordained to
the priesthood is that they will receive from God at
their ordination a light, a warmth; and, for the rest
of us, we pray that within us the embers may be
kindled once again. In this 'crisis of the priesthood',
whatever its explanation, it is important to hang on
to the fact that we have something which cannot be
taken from us. We have received a dynamic force in
which, in the modern world, we must come increasingly
to believe, so that we can, according to the principles
of *Gaudium et spes* and the understanding of *Lumen
gentium*, make our contribution to the world through
the priesthood of Christ.

29. 6. 71

III

Renewal of Vows

1. Offering

I WISH, FATHERS, that this ceremony of the Renewal of Vows could take place during the sacrifice of the Mass.[1] It would remind us of the association between our offerings and that of our Lord. It would re-enact the circumstances of our first Profession, especially the gesture whereby we placed our vows upon the altar on which that sacrifice was offered. It would underline too, the character of thanksgiving our offering should always have. In this ceremony in which we are now engaged, make sure that the renewal of your vows is a genuine offering of self to God, along with the entire work which is to be yours in the years to come.

There are two aspects concerning our offering, which I would like to emphasise.

First, there is no human life which does not, in some respect, share in the Cross of Christ. For those destined to follow Christ there is no escape from the necessity of carrying the Cross. If this is true of human life in general, how much more is it true of those called to follow him in the monastic way. In each one of our lives there are circumstances which inevitably cause some measure of suffering. This may be caused by temperament, relations with others, problems of obedience; but there is no monastic life without some degree of sorrow which, if it is to be fruitful, must be seen as carrying the Cross. This, then, it seems to me, is an admirable opportunity, in offering ourselves, to accept whole-heartedly and gratefully the difficulties which must come our way; and to accept them joyfully, even (dare I say it?) with enthusiasm.

[1] Renewal of vows can now take place during Mass.

Secondly, in offering ourselves to God it is important to offer ourselves as we are—not anxious about what we would wish to be or about gifts not given to us, but ourselves as we are here and now.

Again, we should offer ourselves in thanksgiving for what we find in the life of the Community. For there is no doubt in my mind that the four most important things in our lives are to be found at all levels in this Community: obedience, humility, charity, and prayer. To me it has been a source of consolation to see these qualities thriving—and among the younger monks no less than their brethren. It is a good omen for the future.

Further, if the renewal of our offering were made during the sacrifice of the Mass it would underline the communal aspect of our life and our offering of it. This we must never forget: though we are engaged in different activities, though we have different ideas and different temperaments, yet we have attained unity in the one and only thing that can unite us: devoted service to God.

Two things only can ruin a community, and they are constantly emphasised by St. Benedict. I mention them, not because I think we are offenders but because, if we are to preserve a true monastic spirit, we must check, each in himself, any manifestations of these faults: self-will and murmuring. Self-will is a form of pride and from it follows, almost automatically, destructive criticism.

Finally, I would like to say that, to my mind, there is one thing only at which each of us should aim, and that is prayer. That is the *unum necessarium*: the highest form of union with God that we can attain in this world. If each one of us strives constantly to be a man of prayer, it follows that he will be a man of God. And if that is so, this house will be what it should be: a house of God.

7. 9. 64

2. Humility

There are two particular dangers for a priest and a religious. The first is discouragement at one's own inadequacy; the second, a sense of frustration.

Think of the scene in the Gospel describing the calling of St. Matthew—a most unlikely person. He was a tax collector, one of a body of men notoriously dishonest, coupled with sinners, working for a foreign power, seeming to be throwing away all that the Jews held most precious. The Pharisees took exception to our Lord for associating with Matthew and his friends —'publicans and sinners'. And it was to these same Pharisees that Jesus spoke his golden words: 'It is not those who are well who have need of a physician, but those who are sick.'

Far be it from me to make human weakness a kind of mystique, but it is consoling to know that if I am inadequate, ineffective, the divine physician's hand is there to heal. Fitting for us, indeed, is the message sent by Mary and Martha to Jesus: 'Lord, he whom you love is sick.' The Gospel shows us, beyond question, that in a truly Christian attitude there is no place for discouragement or disappointment, in that the realisation of what we are is a constant claim on God.

Furthermore, our daily experience of inadequacy and weakness forces us, in a remarkable way, to be humble; and humility is the basis of the spiritual life —basis in the sense that it is the beginning: since as a result of original sin we tend to be self-centred, self-seeking, and have to learn to become Christ-centred and, through Christ, God-centred, so that our lives may be dedicated to God and not to the exaltation of ourselves.

And if we learn to be humble, we want a *conversio morum*; and we want to express this through a greater detachment from material things, a deeper consecration of our affections and our bodies to God.

We try to solve the problem of frustration by bending and changing circumstances, so as to remove difficulties and obstacles. But the true religious does this by changing not circumstances but himself, by refusing to allow his peace, the depth of his union with God, to be affected by what goes on around him. More than that, he comes to see that the difficulties, the obstructions, which are the source of his frustrations, are not obstacles to union with God but stepping-stones to this union. He sees God working in his life, in the varied circumstances that make up his life: God work-

Frustration....

ing through the conservatism of some, the forwardness of others; the misunderstandings of some, the light shed by others. We have to realise that in community life God is working out his purpose in ways suited to us. But in a true religious there cannot be deep frustration, because frustration is SELF—things that frustrate, yes, but inner frustration, no. That is the deepest meaning of our vow of stability: we throw in our lot with a particular community, making its strength our strength, its weakness our weakness. Thus the whole provides a unity wherein we experience tolerance, broad-mindedness, good humour, and understanding. And this is stability in its deepest sense.

Nothing is more needed in the Church today than an enthusiasm for the things of God. This is difficult to talk about because to some extent enthusiasm and its manifestations depend on temperament, and an artificial demonstration would be out of place. Nevertheless, when renewing our vows we should renew in ourselves the conviction that our life is worthwhile—not be over-anxious about exterior things but treasure our inner secret: union with God and our brethren, in true charity. There must be joy in our service of God (we have a right to this), a peace and a serenity which are the signs of a life with God. Yes, we have a right to this. We owe it to ourselves to be joyful. Above all, it is essential to our work—the boys in our school, the parishioners in our parishes, should catch something of our enthusiasm for the things of God. More than that, they should detect in us an enthusiasm for the life we have vowed to live. They should see us obeying joyfully, they should see us happy in the service of God.

6. 9. 65

3. Stability

Increasingly one sees in the contemporary Church the guiding hand of God. Changes and reforms are coming in. Necessarily there will be a time for adjustment and, attending change, difficulties, anxieties, disappointments. I want to say a word about three sources of anxiety.

The first is instability.
The second is a kind of activism.
The third is worldliness.
The corrective for instability is our vow of stability. The corrective of activism is to give prayer.the priority it should have in our lives. The corrective of worldliness is a right conception of the rôle of poverty.

In the Orders men and women are abandoning the practice of the religious life. Secular priests, too, are forsaking their obligations. Many reasons are given. Some people are facing difficulties concerning their faith. Some are bored. Some think they could serve God better elsewhere. Some, looking back to the origins of their vocation, conclude that theirs was a mistaken judgment. Some are overcome by difficulties of temperament. In the Church today it is easy, in the light of modern insights, to rationalise difficulties: the rôle of conscience for the Christian; the dignity of the human person; the distinction between the religious life and the lay life, and their respective values; the fear of making a judgment without the maturity proper to an adult.

These are not problems in our own *conventus*, but we are only human and the same could happen to us. All religious have an obligation to clarify their thinking on these problems, if only because it is a duty to help their brethren, Indeed the very nature of our vocation is involved.

It is easy to forget the significance of the words: 'I have chosen you; you have not chosen me.' A vocation — being called by God — is not something that happened to us twenty, thirty, or forty years ago. The voice that spoke to us those many years ago still speaks with the same insistence, expecting the same generous response. *Hodie si vocem eius audieritis, nolite obdurare corda vestra.*[1]

When we took our vows we committed ourselves to the service of God. As in marriage, we were prepared to face whatever life had in store. We signed, on the day of our Profession, a blank cheque made payable to the Lord. A solemn promise was given. Irrevocable. No going back. God had called us. And, Fathers, if you have any doubts about your vocation, do not think

[1] Psalm 94 (R. C. editions)=Psalm 95 (Authorised Version).

about it or discuss it until you have knelt in front of the Blessed Sacrament and solemnly renewed your vows.

These defections happen, too, through a failure to understand the rôle of difficulties in a life hidden with Christ in God. I am sometimes amazed at how little is people's understanding of what following our Lord means. 'If you will be my disciple, you must take up your Cross and follow me.' No religious worth his mettle can find this a negative or depressing programme, for the Cross is the key which opens to us the whole mystery of Christ and the Blessed Trinity and, furthermore, draws us into that mystery. St. Paul teaches that there is no resurrection for us unless we share in the sufferings of Christ. And it is surely axiomatic in the spiritual life that we do not come close to God unless we suffer. That is a hard saying. Hence the outburst of Teresa of Avila: 'No wonder, Lord, you have so few friends when you treat them as you do!'

Difficulties are the voice of God speaking to us. God speaks to us through events, through circumstances. And when these are hard to bear he is trying to make us less reliant upon ourselves, teaching us to have more confidence in him. What I am saying now will not, I know, please some of you: the doctrine I am preaching is not fashionable today. But believe me, Fathers, we make a great error in the religious life if we do not learn, if we do not accept in our hearts, that difficulties are not obstacles between God and ourselves—they are the way to him. We make a great mistake if we fail to realise that this carrying of the Cross is totally compatible with peace, serenity, and happiness. Of course, the whole of life is not like that; of course there are joys in the very living of life, in the living of the religious life. But when the Cross is laid upon our shoulders, that is the time to remember what I am now saying, and to embrace it with joy, almost with enthusiasm, as being the certain way—our Lord's own way—to closer union with him.

In this Community We give ourselves to God in a particular way of life, in a particular place, with particular companions. This is our way: in *this* Community, with *this* work, with *these* problems, with *these* shortcomings. The inner meaning of our vow of stability is that we embrace the life as we find it, knowing that this, and not any other, is our way to God. From time to time, for one reason or another, we are overworked, overstrained. In this instance it is right to put one's case before one's Superior. Many of you have done this, and I have been moved by your humility and your common sense. One more point: To live in this Community, with these problems, with these shortcomings does not mean one should not desire change in this or that; but there must be a basic contentment. When religious seek God first and foremost, they find true contentment, whereas if they seek themselves, they become restless and discontented. We must not, then, be deflected from our primary reason in joining the Community: to seek God.

In seeking God, we need constantly to ask ourselves whether prayer has the place in our lives that it should. Do we really think and act as if prayer came first—before anything else whatever? We have, indeed, the advantage of choir—a very considerable advantage. But advantageous though it is, it has, too, its dangers. Dear Fathers, the observances to which we are bound—the saying of the breviary and so forth—will be for us prayerful experiences in so far as we acquire, along with this, the habit of private prayer. Private prayer and spiritual reading, as I have stressed on many occasions, are the two practices which we must hang on to, if we are to give meaning and vitality to the rest of our prayer life.

And at this point I should like to tell the Community that whatever is said or preached elsewhere, I must insist that before and after Mass there should be an adequate preparation and an adequate thanksgiving. It is an error to argue that these are not necessary.

In the modern world, poverty in the Church is of great importance. Moreover, it is necessary to distinguish between the poverty of the individual and that of the community; the whole communal poverty, the poverty of the Church in general, is something about which the Church will have to examine herself very carefully. But here, it is individual poverty about which I would like to say something. There is always a danger in our lives that we can be at fault in the observance of our poverty. I would urge you, each one of you, Fathers and Brothers, to examine your conscience on this matter. The use to which we put money. On what kind of holidays do we spend it? What about the things we acquire which we do not, in fact, need? We can all think of examples—the sort of things that can make us too dependent on creatures and can come easily between ourselves and God. This is a matter which in the present day demands our urgent consideration.

Fathers, we are about to renew our vows. Ours is an inspiring life because every moment of it can provide an opportunity for a closer union with God. Let us therefore cheerfully, joyfully, renew our gift, make our response to a voice which called us not only in the past but is still calling us today.

5. 9. 66

4. Availability

The renewal of vows should be an occasion of our opening up to the prompting and the moving of the Holy Spirit. In the distant past taking monastic vows was often compared to baptism, when in a very special manner the baptised person is opened up to the Spirit. When we take our vows for the first time, and again when we renew them, I like to think that a voice from heaven says to us, as to Christ at his baptism: 'This is my beloved Son.' I like to think, too: 'I am your beloved son in whom you are well pleased.' When we devote ourselves to God, when we live out our vows, that surely is pleasing to our heavenly Father.

What is the purpose of opening up to the Spirit? What is it that makes the Father see in each one of us his beloved Son; enables him to see in us the reflection of his Son, Christ our Lord? It is the purpose, the reason, for all Christ did: that we should love the Lord our God with our whole heart, our whole mind, our whole soul, and our neighbour as ourselves.

When two people are in love there is in each of them a wanting of the other, a needing of the other. A wants B. B needs and wants A. And it is extremely important that each should know that this is true of the other. It is pre-eminently so in married life. It is so in friendship too.

The constancy of God . . . There is surely deep in the heart of each one of us a wanting and a needing of God, and that wanting and

needing of God in us is only there because he himself
wants and needs us. We could never begin to love God
or understand what that might mean if he had not
first loved us. Why God should want and need us is a
mystery. But it is true: otherwise he would not have
created us and life ultimately would have no meaning
for us. It is good to remember that in God there is a
constancy, a consistency of attitude which never changes,
irrespective of what we are or how we act: he never
changes in his wanting us, needing us. We, on the other
hand, are wayward, easily distracted, inconsistent.
That is one reason why there are vows at all. The
marriage vow serves to protect the original love and
enable it to grow. There would be no need, I suggest,
for vows if we had the constancy and the consistency
of God. I would like, therefore, to say something
about our vow of stability, which reflects our attempt
to live the consistency and constancy which is God.

It is characteristic of love that the beloved be dependable: always trustworthy, always pleased to see you,
always welcoming, ever ready to listen, firm as a rock.
God has these qualities, and we have been told to be
perfect as our heavenly Father is perfect. In our
relationship, in our Community life, there must be a
mutual dependability—each trusting completely in the
others; always ready to listen sympathetically; always
welcoming, open to others. Clearly in a community
there will be differences in the strength of the relationships; but we must be perfect as our heavenly Father
is perfect, and strive to foster among us that dependability upon each other which characterises God's love
for us. Each member of the Community must know
that he is needed and wanted by every other member
and must himself need and want each of the others.
The vow of stability roots us in this Community, and
unless its ultimate meaning is to stabilise us in our search
for the love of God and to strengthen the bonds that tie
brother to brother, then that vow is of little value.

As dependability is characteristic of love, so also is
availability—not the availability which is a spare
fifteen minutes between engagements; it is much deeper
than that. It means that I want to share, I want to give,
I want to do something for the other. When we think
of the availability of our Lord, we see how exacting,

how demanding, availability to others can be. God
has that kind of availability, and Christ is the sacrament
of God's availability. We must model ourselves on
Christ and be perfect as our heavenly Father is perfect
—be available to God and available to one another.
I want to share, I want to give. 'Not my will be done,
but yours' is echoed by our Lady's 'Be it done to me
according to your will'.

It is on these lines that I would like to think tonight
about obedience. My obedience is a sign of my availability, not necessarily in terms only of action, of doing
—which the words 'sharing' and 'giving' connotate—
but also in terms of accepting, of being prepared to
accept God's will even if it means being passed over,
being asked to relinquish some responsibility; or just
being forgotten. Obedience viewed from this angle is
also the constant corrective to my non-availability.
What is it that makes me hesitate to share, hesitate to
give, hesitate to be open? What is it that makes me
hesitate to allow myself to be loved? Often it is our
inhibitions, which can hide selfishness, self-centredness,
self-seeking. Obedience can be my liberation: it can
free me from self and make me available to others.

Obedience (in the sense in which I am thinking of it
now) is not confined to the precepts of Superiors or the
prescriptions of Constitutions or the like. I am thinking
in terms of day-to-day circumstances—the class to be
taken, the presiding I am called upon to do, the sick-
call, the committee meeting—all demands requiring
me to be ready, to be available. The doorbell of a
presbytery and the bell ringing in our cloister: these
are the voice of God summoning us to be available. To
be able to depend on another, to be available to another
—that is what love means, what monastic life means.

These ideals are lofty and difficult to live—indeed
almost beyond our reach, because in the realities of
everyday life our awareness of God's love is not always
vividly in our minds. Whether it be our brethren or
the people we serve, we are conscious of our defects.
All this area of despondency, inadequacy, a sense of
failure, can do more harm, I think, than anything else to
the spontaneity of our love of God and our neighbour.
And such attitudes are widespread among priests
today. But discouragement is a fact and an experience

which all of us undergo at one time or another. However, let me share with you a word of encouragement. You will have heard me ask on previous occasions whether it is better to stand before the Lord giving a list of one's gifts, talents, and achievements, or to be the 'nobody' at the back of the church who can only beat his breast and say: 'Lord, be merciful to me a sinner.' There is comfort in knowing one has not much to offer, that one has achieved little. Isn't this what St. Benedict is talking about in his chapter on humility? And isn't there deep human wisdom in all this? And have we not divine approbation for this humble attitude, since all I have done is to refer you to our Lord's parable?

So it is in that context, perhaps, that we should think about our vow concerning 'conversion of manners': *conversio morum*. Renewal presupposes, from one angle, an increase in humility, a deep genuine recognition of one's need for God. And when I realise that I need God, then I shall want him. And now we seem to be back where we started. We cannot love until we are humble, and we cannot love unless God takes the initiative. Maybe all we can achieve is to become humble. And if we are humble, then the Spirit can take over.

28. 8. 72

5. *Conversio Morum*

It is good, Fathers, to be together during these days. Moreover, I see the events of these twenty-four hours as one. Our Conventual Mass tomorrow is the high point, and this renewal of our vows is part of that Mass, and from that central act devolve our discussions and decisions.

The importance of this renewal of our vows is evident to us all because this is the moment when we strive to rediscover the ideals which prompted us to become monks and commit ourselves for life. It is the moment to recapture our youthful generosity in the service of God: to try, too, to experience anew that wonderful freedom which was ours at the moment in which we declared before God and his saints that we would serve him in the monastery right to the end.

It is the time to evaluate the great monastic vows of stability, *conversio morum*, and obedience. Our adherence to and involvement in this monastic family, with all its strength and weakness, with its future, which is known to God alone and may be different from anything which we could conceive; that *conversio morum* which prompts us to act and react and think as truly befits monks: these characterise our way of life, along with our obedience which is the real proof of our love for God, as indeed between lovers a mutual obedience is a sign of genuine, authentic self-giving.

Monasticism is a 'way of life', and the word 'way' recalls the pilgrim character of this life and of our monastic history. The scene changes, at one period slowly, at another rapidly. We ourselves change and must change. Sometimes our pace will be quick and sure, sometimes it is slow and the going heavy. This is a moment in the year when, by mutual encouragement and example and by the genuine affection we have for one another, the pace can quicken, the step be more certain. It is true—and on such an occasion as this it is appropriate to remind ourselves—that our progress along the road can be delayed by our turning aside and following some byway. I would like to remind you of some of these byways, because each can be, and should be, corrected by the vows we have taken.

We live in a restless age, a restless society. But what period in history has not been much the same? Perhaps we are more aware of this phenomenon in our day; but it is important, if we feel restless, for whatever reason, to recognise that this is an obstacle between ourselves and our service of God. To learn the art of being rightly and properly critical of what we are and what we do, while at the same time remaining wholeheartedly dedicated to the work in hand and to one another; to preserve an inner peace while being at the same time aware of the voice of the Spirit speaking to us individually or collectively so as to lead us along ways unknown and unforeseen; to be aware of the call of the Spirit in the needs of our times; to be aware of the call of the Church and at the same time to be at peace, at rest: this is possible only if our pursuit is single-minded and constant. The way which we can follow all too easily is the one in search of 'self'. I have no need to remind you of this. St. Benedict reminds us how pernicious it can be. 'Love seeketh not her own.'

There are simple tests by which we can discover *God or* whether our heart is set on God or whether we are pre- *self?...* occupied with self. To take some examples. How do I react when I am asked to lay down one task and take up another; when work that might have come my way is assigned to someone else; when I am required to do something one way when I wanted to do it another; when I let myself feel frustrated because my ideas have not been followed, my ideals not recognised? No need to labour the point.

Another byway is worldliness. This is difficult to define. It is in the heart and mind rather than in what we do. What, we might ask, is our attitude when we are away from the monastery? Looking back on a holiday, can we say we have always been proud to be monks? Or have we tried to emancipate ourselves from our monasticism by our behaviour or by the clothes we wear? Enjoy being a monk. Be proud to be a monk.

What keeps us on our path? What deters us from turning down byways? What is the over-riding concern of each one of us? The question provides the answer. In our hearts we know that it is in pursuit of the love of God that we shall not only fulfil ourselves in our monastic vocation but attain true stature as human beings. We should ponder often on the graciousness and the lovableness of God—especially the graciousness and lovableness of his Incarnate Son, through whom he speaks to us. Pondering on the life of Christ as a revelation of God's love, seeing and understanding it in that light; pondering on the beauty of God's creation and on all that is noblest and best in man's attainments; pondering, too, on the lovableness of other people—there we have the key which will unlock the mystery of the love that is God. What fear is it, what hesitation prompted by fear, that makes us diffident as to the reactions to which we are entitled in the face of the beauty and the wonderful qualities in others? In all that we experience, all that we know, let us find, at least seek, the love of God. Words are not adequate, but allow me to quote the mystic Julian of Norwich:

'The love of God most high for our soul is so wonderful that it surpasses all knowledge. No created
being can know the greatness, the tenderness, the
love our Maker has for us. By his grace and help,
therefore, let us in spirit stand and gaze, eternally
marvelling at the supreme, surpassing, single-minded,
incalculable love that God, through his goodness,
has for us. Then we can ask reverently of our Lover
whatever we will, for, by nature, our will wants God
and the goodwill of God wants us. We can never
cease wanting and longing until we possess him in
fulness of joy: then we shall have no further want.
Meanwhile his will is that we go on knowing and
loving until we are perfected in Heaven.'[1]

That mystical English tradition, I like to think, was
influential at the time of the re-foundation of our
Congregation, and it has such a marvellous relevance
to what people are seeking today that we would do
well to read and follow this teaching, and acquire
something of this outlook.

You will bear with me if I recall, as on many previous
occasions, another tradition that is very much part of
us: the tradition of the martyrs. It is foolish, and also
wrong, to forget that the way to God must be at one
period or another that of the Cross. It is unfair to those
with whom we have dealings to hide from them this
reality. The Gospel is clear. The tradition that comes
down to us is that the Cross is something joyous,
though, when it weighs most heavily, it is far from
being so in our experience. Let me share a thought
with you: whenever any one of us is bowed down by
the weight of the Cross to the extent that this particular
person—whether a monk or otherwise—feels he is not
accepting it, does not want to and cannot, that is truly
the Cross. And if, within, there is the sensation of revolt,
do not be troubled. When it is easy to 'offer up' something, that is not the real thing. Forgive me for labouring this point, but we need, all of us, to know how to
avail ourselves of these situations. We need also, I
believe, to know how to counsel others who find
themselves in a like situation. When the Cross is too
heavy to bear and I fall to the ground; when I do not

[1] *Revelations of Divine Love*, Chapter 6.

want to accept it, that is something really imposed upon us by the Lord. Moreover our true, living faith tells us that this is the way to a new life, a moment of growth. The martyrs went with a glad heart to face their trials. It should be the same for us.

As monks we are heirs to a tradition reaching far back into the past. I was struck by a reading[1] we had in the refectory. I found it impressive because the authors themselves were great men. And to listen to great men admiring and evaluating really noble persons without—as often happens—cutting them down to size, is remarkably refreshing. There is, I think, a lesson there about our charity, our respect for one another, our tolerance. We should always be ready to admire each other, to hold each other in respect; to feel, too, deep concern and deep compassion. After all, our search for God is our response to a love which he has first shown us. And so we can learn from one another and together, as a community, return to him.

We shall now proceed to this moment of renewal of our vows. Let us do so with sincerity, full of hope, knowing that, as we are doing this, Christ is in our midst and the Father looking down upon us in favour: 'Surely these are my beloved sons in whom I am well pleased.'

... in whom I am well pleased ...

27. 8. 73

6. Reassurance

Our Lord once asked a very unusual question: not the kind of question which in ordinary circumstances a man puts to another; indeed, it is a question that probably should never be asked, or at any rate rarely.

The question is: 'Simon, son of John, do you love me more than these?' 'Simon, son of John, do you love me?' And then a third time. St. Peter, disconcerted, finally says: 'Lord, you know all things, you know that I love you.'

It is human to need reassurance, very human. But is it not possibly also divine? I put it as a question, not a statement. I would tremble to call it an insight, for who can know the mystery that is God? And yet, I

[1] *The English Way. Studies in English Sanctity from St. Bede to Newman* by M. C. D'Arcy and others, ed. Maisie Ward, London 1933.

think, the words of Jesus ask you and me to give him an assurance, a reassurance we would hesitate to ask of one another. Nonetheless gestures, sincere and in their way eloquent, are necessary among ourselves. They are also necessary in our relationship with God: a gesture of reassurance to God that I love him, or at least want to do so.

Simon, son of John . . .   Our Lord would not have asked the question if it had not been important to him: if Peter, as a person, had not mattered to him. 'Simon, son of John, do you love me?' This question is put to each one of us. Our answer may reveal that we are disconcerted: 'You know all things, Lord. You know that I love you.' But into our mind crowd all sorts of problems, personal and monastic, and we may wonder whether in other circumstances our answer might have been more truthful. Love does not know the limits of space, time, and circumstance: it is a bond between two people which transcends such things: in richness and poverty, in sickness and health, in times good and bad—the reality endures.

Our Lord says three things in reply to St. Peter's threefold answer. Let us look at them in reverse order. His final command to Peter is: 'Follow me.' Had not Peter already been called? Perhaps this 'calling' after the Resurrection was the definitive, final call. At the first call the atmosphere is quite different; it is more exciting: the Messiah has come, the Kingdom will be restored. 'We have found him', Andrew says. Andrew tells Peter, and the next day Philip is called; after that, Nathaniel. Hopes are high: 'You will see the heavens opening, the angels coming up and down—and the Son of Man.' Boats are abandoned on the shores of Lake Galilee and nets left to dry.

Did Peter feel at times disillusioned? 'We have forsaken everything: what will be our reward?' Those silly arguments about who will be the highest in the Kingdom—those are very human. Peter's idea of the Kingdom was not that of our Lord. But had Peter, as he dragged the boat up the shore, foreseen his new-found hero bowed under another load in supreme humiliation, and foreseen his own despicable behaviour (his running away and his betrayal of his Master), would he so readily have answered 'Yes'? He was a young man full of vigour, hopes and plans: 'Truly, truly, I say to you, when you were young you girded yourself and walked where you would; but when you are old you will stretch out your hands and another will gird you to carry you where you do not wish to go.'[1] Our Lord said this, so it is recorded, to show by what death Peter was to glorify God. St. Paul saw more in it than the physical death that would be Peter's: to St. Paul it was a death which meant life, a daily dying to live more fully. Not the crushing of vigour and plans, but their transformation into God's vigour, God's plans: 'When you were young you girded yourself and walked where you would; but when you are old you will stretch out your hands and another will gird you to carry you where you do not wish to go.'

The Kingdom is not what we suppose it to be or what we wish it to be: it is God's Kingdom and comes *his* way, not ours. And Peter must become small: you will not be effective unless you love, and that is why he was asked three times. The reassurance was given: 'You know all things, Lord. You know that I love you.' Now the command is given, the task entrusted: 'Feed my sheep.' Give them hope, give them joy, give them freedom, give them life, give them Christ. They have not the same hopes, but each must still hope; not all have joy, but each has a right to it; they all want life, and life more abundantly; they must love one another as I, the Lord, have loved you. So all things work together for good. Our task is to strive to love him and all those who matter to him, and to feed his sheep.

The question is put to you and to me: 'Do you love me?' and our reply is: 'You know all things, Lord, you know that I love you.' Give the reassurance in spite of yourselves, whatever your troubles, your aspirations, your differences, your failings: they are of little account in comparison to that vocation to love, which is the Christian call. In renewing your Profession, give that reassurance to God that you want to return love first given to us. When all is said and done, this is the one thing that matters.

25. 8. 75

[1] John 21:18.

IV

Monastic work

1. Activity

LAST TIME I WAS talking to you about change and
discussions going on today in the Church, in the field
of education and in monasticism. I said that I thought
this unrest will last for many years; that we are bound
for a considerable time to live through a very unsettled
period. This poses a problem for the individual. And I
tried to stress the importance of not allowing things
under discussion (they may modify our way of life)
to disturb the inner peace of each individual or the
peace of the Community. I pointed out that we must
learn to accept the present situation in which each one
of us finds himself, whether it be uncongenial tasks,
personal problems, or ideas which are not recognised.
I emphasised the importance of recognising the Cross
when it comes our way and, finally, of having limitless
trust and confidence in God.

We live in a restless age. We question and criticise
every aspect, almost, of the Church's life and the religious life, too. Good, honest criticism is healthy. But
it is bad if it unsettles the individual or leads to strain.
There is another byproduct of criticism and questioning
which can be harmful to the individual's spiritual life
and therefore to that of the Community. It is what
St. Benedict, as I have reminded you on previous
occasions, calls 'murmuring'. In the Rule St. Benedict
warns us time and again against murmuring. 'Obedience', he says, 'will only be acceptable to God and
sweet to men if what is commanded is carried out not
fearfully, tardily, or coldly, or with murmuring, nor
with an answer showing unwillingness.' Again, the
waiters are to carry out their orders without murmuring.

As to the amount of wine we drink and so forth: as to this, we 'admonish above all that there be no murmuring among them'. Again, when he discusses the question of uniformity of treatment for all, he says: 'Let not the evil of murmuring show itself by the slightest word or sign, on any account whatever.' Lest you think it is all weighed in one direction, let me read this passage: 'Let the Abbot so arrange and dispose all things that souls may be saved, that the brethren may do what they have to do without just cause for murmuring.' And of course St. Benedict, with his great emphasis on consultation and so forth, recognises the probability — or the desirability — of criticism being made and being voiced, but without bitterness or a wrong kind of zeal. Murmuring is detrimental to the spiritual life. It betrays non-acceptance of the present situation: and the present situation in which we find ourselves is the one in which God wants us to be.

There is today much talk concerning the distinction to be made between the religious life as such and the clerical life. It is true that one does not have to be a priest in order to be a religious, but religious are suitable persons to be priests. This has always been our tradition. Ours (I am talking about the English Benedictines) has always been an active Congregation — or I prefer the word 'mixed': contemplation and activity. Historically speaking, we have never really worked that one out. Monastic life has developed over the years, with its choir duties and so forth. And running a school has also developed. But I think that if these two are going to fit more easily into each other, then there will have to be some modification: I am an advocate of some modification being made to the monastic observance, so as to relieve tensions which can exist between a full-scale monastic life and full-scale school activity. There are many schemes abroad today for shortening the Office,[1] for making monastic observance simpler. I am in favour of this in so far as it will dovetail prayer and work in a more balanced manner.

Our life is one in which we engage in activity, and our activity is apostolic. I am not impressed with the view *A stepping-stone to God . . .*

[1] In 1965 the Full Latin Breviary was still in use as the Monastic Office. For example Sunday Matins lasted ninety-five minutes without a break. In the New English Office, this was shortened to thirty minutes.

of monasticism which starts from the premise that it is a 'flight from the world'. Historically this 'flight' idea came in fairly late—I should say towards the end of the third century. In the Gospels and the Acts of the Apostles the ideal was the apostolic life. (Again I do not want to be held to this thesis—but it is worth consideration. For myself, I would never have come to this Community if there had not been parishes.) Whatever the future holds for us, we ought to be clear that our forefathers have handed on to us something extremely precious. Those who have gone before us have grown holy in this life, and have done great work for God both in our schools and in our parishes. And there is no doubt that the work we do in the school and in parishes is not only worthwhile in itself but immensely profitable to our souls. Dealing with other people—whether schoolboys or parishioners—helping others is found to be one of the most powerful ways of drawing closer to God. It would be difficult to explain how this works, but it is the experience of a great number of persons. Our twofold work is extremely satisfying, and that is something which is precious, because all through our life we are blessed with the knowledge that we are doing something worthwhile in itself, profitable to ourselves, and by and large congenial. For although it is true that one must see the Cross when it comes and accept it, work, on the other hand, must be ·congenial and satisfying if the spiritual life is to develop normally: it cannot be all Cross and austerity.

The point I want to make is that our work, by its very nature, draws us closer to God and is, for us individually, immensely beneficial. I am not talking about the enormous contribution our work makes to the Church; I am simply saying that each moment of the day provides an opportunity for us to come closer to God. A difficulty, a problem, is not, as it may at first seem, a stumbling-block. On the contrary, it is a stepping-stone on our way to God.

19. 5. 65

2. Schoolmaster

The beginning of term provides an opportunity to give

you some basic thoughts concerning the school. I cannot, as Abbot, abandon my interest in the school or my responsibility for it. On the contrary, it is my task to make sure that the school is making the maximum contribution to the life of the Church in this country. At the present time there are two points which need to be emphasised.

First, we must take stock and consider very carefully what we are doing to teach and train boys in the practice of their religion, and thus fit them for life in the world. Basic principles remain the same—but this is 1966, not 1930 or 1920.

Secondly, we have to consider how we can make boys learn to work on their own. We would all, I think, question whether in the past we have been a hundred per cent successful in that sphere. The art of schoolmastering can be summed up quite simply: it is to teach boys to teach themselves—to teach boys to teach themselves how to live, how to pray, how to work, how to direct their lives, how to shoulder responsibility and so forth. And we have to learn how much we can leave to the boys and how much we need to intervene to keep the balance. The balance implies knowing what is going on—how much we can leave to the boys and at what point we need to take the reins into our own hands. The balance means knowing what is going on, taking action in some cases and in others refraining from doing so.

Schoolmastering is a difficult art and also a noble one. It is difficult to the extent that we must be beginners all the time. Reflecting on my own experience, I would now do many things in quite a different way. But it is an art, and one that has to be learnt, in part from experience, in part from those who have already had experience. And this is very important. My housemastering I learnt from the other seven housemasters —as it was then. When we are young on the staff, we have to be sensitive to the experience (and there is a great deal of experience in the Community) of those who have preceded us.

I will just add that a great source of pride in our school is the relationship which we have established with the boys. This is indeed something precious and we have got it right: we learned it from those who went

A precious relation- ship . . .

before us. They established a wonderful relationship and a balance which we have inherited. But it is something we need to watch, protect, and treasure. We have to strike a happy balance—be on our guard against over-familiarity, becoming 'one of the boys', thus winning a spurious success. A certain detachment, a certain self-control, a capacity to say 'No' to oneself yet retain warmth and friendship—here is to be found the key to so much we can do for the boys. But ours is a precious tradition which could easily go wrong.

Just as the Abbot cannot run the school and consequently delegates it to the Headmaster, so the Headmaster cannot run every department. He too must delegate. But let us remember that basically it is the Headmaster who runs the school, and this he does through a team. But the team is hierarchically organised: housemasters, senior masters and other officials. But they—the housemasters, senior masters and other officials—must know when to refer things to the Headmaster. They must know when things are going on which should be passed on to the Headmaster: and they should err on the side of telling too much rather than too little.

Naturally, there are things which cannot be passed on; things, for example, heard under the seal of confession—a clear case. Also things which would be classed as 'committed secrets'. But school work is team work: the whole Community must feel corporately and collectively responsible for all that goes on in the school. The Community must be made to feel that they are part of the 'show'. As I say, the school is organised hierarchically, because in an enormous venture of this sort it could not be otherwise; but everyone has a part to play, everyone a contribution to make. Everybody's ideas and opinions are important and should be listened to. The Headmaster welcomes members of the Community and of all his staff who go to talk to him about the school and its problems, but he is a very busy man. I have not discussed this point with him, but I am sure I am saying what he would want me to say—that, although he is very busy, no one should use this as a reason for not worrying him: if you have something to say to him or something you want to hear from him, you should go. I am always frightened when people say: 'Oh, the Abbot is terribly busy, we must not worry him.' That is not right. If the Abbot should be worried, then he must be. And it is the same with the Headmaster.

As we face the new term, several people have to be out of the monastery, absent from choir and away from the routine of our life as monks. When I was a Junior and a young priest I used to think: 'Well, there they go. This is the end of their monastic life until Christmas Eve; and anyway, they will probably go away then.' And then I learnt that it is not like that at all.

The model for a house here is the monastery. The housemaster, in a sense, is rather like the Abbot, living in his community—the house. Why? To teach the boys to be committed Christians; also the art of living in community. That is what he is trying to do for his sixty or so boys. That is why he is there with them. I liked to think, when I said my Office, that this was the little community's particular share in the Church's praise of God—the community whose centre is the house Mass and community prayers. I used to think that the model was the twelve Benedictine monasteries at Subiaco. I hope this is not naïve or fanciful, but it meant much to me—and it made sense. I was, as the father of this little community, teaching its members to live the Christian life and to be members of a community. I was there as their priest, as if presiding over a small parish. And that is why I have always been against the idea of the whole school attending Mass in one place, all at the same time.

Some have to be out of choir because our duties call us away. In an ideal monastery, in an ideal world, we would all be able to attend choir and then all be able to carry out our monastic tasks. This is indeed an ideal of which we should never lose sight; but in the meanwhile the onus is on the individual to play his part, as far as is possible, in the monastic choir. The Conventual Mass is a good example. For it is my view that, ideally, the whole conventus should be present at this Mass. I hope that one day this will be possible. As it is, though we cannot always attend, it remains the corporate responsibiliy of the whole Community that this, the centre of the monastic day, should be celebrated worthily and in as dignified a way as befits an act done for the honour and glory of God. So I would urge you, Fathers, that when you have your timetable you go through it, each one of you, and note the days when you can in all honesty attend the Conventual Mass, even at some inconvenience or at the cost of an extra effort at another time of the day. You may be able to pick only one day, or possibly two or three, but decide that at those times you are going to be at the Conventual Mass, and stick to it. If everyone takes this view—that the Conventual Mass is our corporate responsibility—then we shall have our principles right.

There are practical reasons for this, apart from the principle itself, since in this particular year it is going to be difficult to keep things going. But there is another principle now for cantors. I have discussed this with the Headmaster and we have agreed that when the work is allocated by him and the senior masters, certain Fathers should be available on certain days to provide for the singing. And so, instead of the responsibility for attendance at Conventual Mass being left to the Abbot and Prior, and their having to chase people up, it is now—and always was or should have been—the corporate responsibility of the whole body.

Corporate responsi- bility . . .

I must now go on to some particular points, but before doing so I would like to quote St. Benedict: 'Therefore we must establish a school of the Lord's service, in founding which we hope to ordain nothing harsh or burdensome. But if for a good reason, for the amendment of an evil habit or for the preservation of charity, there be some strictness of discipline, do not be dismayed and flee from the way of salvation, of which the entrance must needs be narrow.' I do not like great lists of rules. On the other hand, for the preservation of charity and discipline—that is, for the smooth running of the establishment—it is necessary that we be clear on certain points. But the spirit behind these is rather like the spirit behind the Conventual Mass: it is our corporate responsibility.

A last point. I have been perturbed these last three years and have not known quite what to do about it, by the number of you who go away, during the year, at Christmas and at Easter. For the efficient running of the school it is necessary to go away on courses, for science masters' meetings, and so forth. People also need to take school parties. This is highly desirable. And, quite frankly, some people need to go away — just to be away. I recognise all this and I do not want to prejudice either the efficient running of the school or the health of the brethren. But having said this, I wish we could learn to relax here, more than we do, during holidays, and feel that withdrawing into the monastery, attending choir, and taking life at a more leisurely pace can itself be relaxing. We can get into a state of mind in which we cannot relax unless we are away, and this is bad for us. And it is not good for the Community: for it is extraordinary how we are never together, and misunderstandings arise simply because people are not here. If you are away most of the Christmas holidays and most of the Easter holidays, and all August, it is easy to get out of touch with what people are thinking, what is worrying them and so on. And this applies especially to housemasters and others immersed in school: they do not provide an opportunity for younger members of the Community to get to know them. It should be a two-way traffic.

I cannot lay down rules or principles about this. How to tackle the problem baffles me. But perhaps we can all think about it and be less ready, perhaps, to want to go away. Again, it is not a question of rules and regulations: it is a question of the spirit of the thing — and the expectation, dear Fathers, that from now on you might get the answer 'No' and not 'Yes'!

Schoolmastering, like much we do for God, is 'iceberg work'. Very little, perhaps, appears on the surface, but deep down, under the surface, something is going on which is very, very important in a boy's life. The very contact with men who are committed to God and are known to be committed to him and are seen to be, is of more value than all we say or do. Boys are very perspicacious: they are very much more shrewd than we think, and they know whether the man who is looking after them or with whom they have dealings is genuine or not. Little things can have a tremendous effect on boys. Years later a man of, say, twenty-five will meet you and say: 'I always remember the first thing you said to me. I arrived very nervous and worried about coming to school, and you said . . .'

You probably didn't say it, or you have forgotten, or it was something very trivial. But that is what one discovers in schoolmastering: it is the hundred-and-one things one says or does which have an importance and effect out of all proportion. That is why schoolmastering is worthwhile: for everything helps towards building up a life. It is what we are that matters. It is the small things that count.

A bell goes for Monastic Choir Office. And if I go on talking about whether it ought to be so-and-so or so-and-so at scrum-half tomorrow, or whether we ought to wear denims or not, that is not as convincing as obedience to the bell. When the boys see that, as monks, we are disciplined and want to lead our monastic life fully, this makes a greater impact than running round in circles. It is what they see us to be that is important.

And so, dear Fathers, we can only be men of God if we are men of prayer. Let us be men of prayer, and then we will be good monks and, necessarily, good schoolmasters.

7. 9. 66

3 '. . . contemplata aliis tradere . . .'

The monastic life is, above all else, a search for God. It is not the acquiring of virtues, or the fostering of moral integrity; it is not carrying the Cross, it is not going flat-out at work; it is not living under obedience; it does not provide an environment for an individual to discover himself and work at his own spirituality. Any one of these would constitute a partial vision of what monasticism is. They are component parts; but they are means, not ends. The end is the search for union with God. In our pastoral work our task as monks is (in a phrase I used at the Renewal of Vows) *contemplata aliis tradere* – to hand on to others things which have been contemplated.

Contemplation is not just looking at God; for most of us, now *in via*, it consists in looking *for* God, and if from time to time some 'sight' of him is accorded, this will only be a glimmer granted by grace in what will always be a 'cloud of unknowing'. So when I use the term 'contemplation' I use it in this sense: looking for God. This looking for God is done through, with, and in Christ, in unity with the Holy Spirit so that we can give, within that very life of the Trinity, all honour and glory to God, the Almighty Father. That in brief is, I think, the essence of the monastic life.

It is a search for God in community. This is a value which has been emphasised in recent years, and rightly so. And although I think it is true that we have in the past been justly proud of our charity as a community, nevertheless we shall need to an increasing degree a sense of community, an awareness of community, an involvement in community. Yes, ours is a search for God in community, and it is in the light of that idea that I would like to propose some liturgical changes in our way of life. These are in the nature of relaxations in one sense, but rationalisations in another, and I think they are to be justified. Today there is a stirring in the Church—of that I am certain; and I am quite convinced that in a year or two there will be a great number of vocations to the religious life. I am equally certain— totally convinced—that young people will not join the monastery unless there is a distinctive challenge, and, if I may say so, the life is seen to be one that is worth-while, in which a man can dedicate himself and in which there is an element of sacrifice. Harm has been done in religious life in the last few years by thinking that renewal is to some degree co-extensive with per-missiveness and a general slackening. This has been a grave error.

Our choral prayer is important, and as you know, some of us have been participating in group prayer, and this, I am sure, is a thing for the future: it is certainly a thing for the present. One of the reasons why I introduced it is because the world is going to have to learn how to pray, and I do not think that modern man will be made to pray through sermons: he will be taught to pray by being made to pray, and he will only be made to pray if he is praying with some-body else initially. And I think that it is groups of people praying together which is going to spread, as it were, the prayer 'thing'. This is one reason why we ought to do it—to try to understand what happens, and make our mistakes. When we open our mouths

Group prayer . . .

in our group praying, we have not yet discovered, I think, the way to do it, but I believe we have all opened our mouths enough, including myself, to know what *not* to say! We should *not* be preaching homilies to each other; we should *not* be having a communal pricking of conscience; we should *not* be indulging in group therapy; we should *not* be discovering ourselves at depth; we should *not* be orientating God to us; we should *not* be limiting our vision of God to somebody who is 'up there' in order to see us through today. What is our prayer? It is a search for God in community, essentially in silence. I think harm has been done by a failure to see that prayer is, in the first instance, a waiting upon God in silence. This I think is very much what monastic prayer should be. When people open their mouths during this kind of prayer it is to break the silence in order to prepare for the next silence.

What we need is people to say what aspect of God, or what aspect of Christian life, strikes them, so as to illuminate and help the rest of the group. This must be theocentric, Christocentric, rather than a little group concerned with its own small world, its own problems. We have done a good job, and I think that it is going to pay off for a number of us. Above all, I think it will help us to rediscover the 'soul' of communal vocal prayer.

Our life is community prayer; our life is community work. I have come to see more and more clearly that there is a danger in monastic writers who play down 'work'. After all, if you think of what we are doing when working, we are participating in the creative act of God. And that is a wonderful thing. And what is more creative than education? What is more creative, more Godlike, than to imprint the image of his Son on another person? And that is what we are doing. What could be more creative than getting a young person just to learn and to know—for the more I know, the more I am sharing in God's mind; just as the more I love, the more I am sharing in the activity of God's love. And so, at a very high level, we have to see our monastic work as a participation in the creativity of God himself. So I would urge you to be guided by this vital truth in all your thinking about your work.

I do not believe that God will bless a monastic

community which is not obedient; I do not believe that the work of an individual will be blessed if it is not done in accordance with obedience. It certainly will not be blessed if it goes counter to the wishes which have been expressed by a Superior, however wrong or short-sighted he may be. When we became monks we knew that we would be ruled by men with limitations; temperamental, intellectual, and the rest. This is what we took on; we knew it. And believe me, the older you get the more surprised you become regarding your contemporaries in positions of authority, and how limited they really are. That is a fact. I am saying this, not because we are all bad at it; but a bad doctrine can get in and spread quickly, and I want to be quite certain that it does not do so here. For instance, the doctrine that if a Superior really knew all the circumstances he would not have commanded as he did, and so I am free to disregard him: that, I think, is wrong. Another error is that a command given can only be carried out within the whole context of what has to be done. Again that seems reasonable, but it is dangerous. Then there is the doctrine that the law of charity must always prevail over rules of obedience. This is very dangerous, because it can be true. What I am trying to say is that it will be very rare, or should be very rare, when we decide that the law of charity must prevail over the regulations.

To continue on this question of obedience. I would remind you, Fathers, that what I have said must not be, of course, with any prejudice to the use of initiative or common sense. I would much prefer a person to be disobedient than to whittle down obedience; much rather that one be honest and say: 'I am just jolly well not going to do it,' than to whittle down the doctrine. I have come more and more to see just how central is obedience in the religious life. An obedient religious has acquired an interior freedom. Always see obedience as liberating, and a conforming to Christ.

A postscript on the arranging of work. Job definition in industry, or whatever, is normally not done by the one who is being employed: a man is normally employed to do a job defined by somebody else. And in industry and commerce it is expected that the individual will use initiative, have scope, have freedom. But you cannot run a place efficiently — just to put it at that level — unless people are prepared to do their job in the way in which authority indicates. And when there is a clash between what you think and what authority thinks, then in the interests of efficiency (apart from anything else) one has to yield to another's view. Often people develop their work in a way in which higher authority does not know, or may not want, and so one has to be sensitive about asking whether this is what is wanted. At a deeper level, if we try to plan our own lives, make our own lives, carry out our work as we please, we can smother that total availability, that surrender, which is the ultimate liberation of our mind and the sign that the love of God is dwelling in us. Availability and surrender should mean not force, not pain, not agony, not struggle, but joy because ultimately I am not seeking myself, not forwarding my own interests, but seeking the Lord. If we get it right in our prayer life, right in our hearts, it follows that we shall get it right in our practice. Then we shall not be competitive in our work; shall not be using our work to climb; not using our work to advertise ourselves, nor to find our fulfilment in it, because our treasure lies elsewhere.

This is a high ideal which I have been putting before you, Fathers, and I look back in sorrow and trepidation at my having the nerve to say this to you — I who have made these obvious mistakes all through my life. Perhaps it is because one has made the mistakes that one can look back and see the pity it was. But what I want to leave with you is this tremendous vision of work as being a sharing in the creativity of God. And that should be pondered. The powers that I have, whatever they are, are powers that are sustained by God, and I am acting as a divine instrument in order to fashion what he would have me fashion. This is a tremendous thought, and there is no higher way of doing this than by educating, by communicating; and there is nothing higher in educating than to convey to others a sense of God. That is what our life is: *contemplata aliis tradere.*[1]

6. 9. 71

---

[1] St. Thomas II II Q188 a6.

4. Devotedness

I have been thinking about renewal, monastic renewal. Whereas, on the one hand, it would be odious to be complacent about our life here, yet one has to recognise that there are a number of things which work well. Again, it would be odious to be over-critical of the way renewal takes place in other monasteries or religious Orders. But I do think, as I have suggested earlier, that in many cases communities are in danger of making a very grave mistake by going too quickly in what one might call a permissive direction. Those who have consciously tried to make life easier for their members are making, I think, a grave mistake. There certainly is, I believe, a correlation between recruitment and the demands which an Order makes on its members. I shall try, presently, to explain what I think that demand amounts to. And as far as we are concerned, there is one guiding principle which I can trust: that whatever we do, whatever we plan, however much we change, there are these five things to which we must be faithful if we are to remain something of what we have been—if, indeed, we are to continue at all. I have mentioned these before, but I make no apology for doing so again, so important are they: prayer, obedience, hard work, community life, poverty. Those are the essential, basic qualities which our monastic life must have.

Moreover, a challenging question has been put to me twice in the last ten days by persons who are drawn to the monastic life—indeed, admire it. The question they put, the hesitation they feel, the problem in their mind, amounts to: 'Haven't you, in a sense, opted out; created for yourselves a pleasant environment in which you are largely spared the kind of responsibilities which we have to carry as we battle through everyday life?' My mind turns to X, ten years married, married rather late in life, father of five children; on the verge of being made redundant at the age of nearly fifty, weighed down with anxieties and problems. Or Y, bedevilled by ill-health, aware that he has made a mistake in his married life and will have to spend the rest of his days with an incompatible wife, and she with an incompatible husband. Or Z, who holds down a job which he does not like, finds it a great trial; cannot change at his age; has a handicapped child. Why X Y Z? We have similar cases in our own families, most of us; and indeed, when you come to think of it, X Y and Z might have been you and I. Yes, when the question is put, these examples (which can be multiplied over and over again) come to mind.

My answer is: Yes, we have many advantages: we are assured of three meals a day, we have a roof over our heads, we are clothed, we live in congenial company, we have security for our old age. And then I go on to say that there can only be one justification for our being given by God these wonderful things, these great advantages, when the majority of mankind does not share them. It can only be justified, I say, on the grounds that we are living a life that makes demands on us as the ordinary processes of living make demands on you. And in our monastic life the two areas in which the demands are made are in our prayer life and in our work. Prayer makes its demands, and the more responsible a prayer life is, the more demands are made through it by the Lord. And work makes its demands because we work long hours: we work intensely, we work seven days out of seven. And even when we are not engaged in working at quite the same pressure, we still have to carry out our obligations: choir Office. And there are the claims of the traditional vows of chastity, poverty, and obedience.

In the early years of the monastic life it is the small things which seem to weigh, but later, the big things. Chastity, poverty and obedience can be greater trials later than they are early on. And then I begin to wonder whether this is convincing. There is a nasty kind of nagging at the back of my mind that maybe that is the way it ought to be—but, in my case, sadly is not.

All that I have mentioned: the claims of the vows and the demands made by our activities, can present us with the same possibilities of heroism or dogged courageousness which people in the world have to elicit in themselves through the circumstances of their lives. Sometimes I ask myself, why must the human life have demands made upon it? Then I remember the shudders that we get when we talk about the

difficulties of the monastic life, or when the Cross is
mentioned, and we recognise that life, a monastic life,
built on a kind of spiritual masochism, would be a
distortion of what monasticism should be. We recognise in ourselves a curious, lurking spectre, deep in
the spirit, when we feel that somehow if things were
going well there must be something wrong; or if life
isn't grim it cannot be good! That, too, is a spectre
which must be exorcised: you cannot base a human
life, or monastic life, on that! There is, too, ingrained
in us a feeling (a feeling, not a rational thing) that the
more we do the more virtuous we are; the more prayers
we say the more virtuous we are, and so on. That
principle is untheological; nor has it any basis in
Scripture or tradition. As we know, the principle of
merit is charity, not the quantity of the things we do,
endure, or say in our prayers. Yes, the principle of
merit is charity. But having said that, it has to be
admitted that devotion to prayer and to work is a sign
of charity, a sign of life.

I am certain of the vital rôle which work plays in
our monastic way of life. Without work we shall cease
to be what we have been, and further, we shall cease to
be. And work done by the brethren is not an escape
from self into activity (it can be that); nor is it a ladder
to be climbed in the nature of a career. It is our sharing
in God's creativity; the flowing, in activity, of our love
for our Lord and Master, and our neighbour. It is a
selfless devotion to those whom we serve in the school,
in the parishes and elsewhere. We remember with
admiration—to single out one monk from our past—
Fr. Stephen Marwood: so obviously a man of God, a
man who had reached a very high level of prayer, and
yet, among us, was one of the busiest and most devoted
of the brethren. To this day people quote him as having
had a profound influence. And he was representative,
I think—and he was only one—of the finest type of
monk which this house has produced. As I say, I am
only taking him as representative. I could have mentioned other names, but he was outstanding—so fully
a human being, so eminently human and humane.

*Human and
humane . . .*

And if I go on to talk about being human in the
monastic life—I say this not in reproach, not implying
that we have not these qualities—I like to think that

the things about which I am going to talk are a description of what we are trying to be and what most of us, some of the time, are. But the gentler qualities—if one might put it that way—are important: being considerate, thoughtful, available, dependable, co-operative, helpful, cheerful, accepted and accepting; sensitive to others, forgiving, generous, unselfish. Well, we all have our list of qualities—what we think would make a fine human being and a fine monk—and I don't think any of us would leave out any of those qualities. But there remain for all of us tremendous ideals: consideration, forgiveness, unselfishness, generosity. These are the gentler qualities, the appealing qualities, without which no life is truly human and no monastic life tolerable. But a monastic life must also give to the monk a sense of responsibility, and here I would refer to three points.

First, I must be able to commit myself to my vocation for the whole of my life; and having committed myself, stick it out through thick and thin. And people, young people, are on the whole hesitant to take this step. But the longer I live the more I realise that the hesitation is a sign of immaturity, because there comes a point where one has to be able to take a responsible step of this sort and stick to it, come what may. I met the other day a woman in her seventies. She has had and is having a dreadful life (she is not a Catholic)—a *dreadful* life with a cantankerous and, I would say, somewhat unbalanced husband. She said: 'I could leave him, Father, I could; but I won't because of my vows.' Such was her loyalty and devotion to a promise, made some fifty years ago, which had brought her little pleasure, little joy.

There is another form of that responsibility, or that responsible quality, which I would like to put before you: dependability. You are not a responsible person unless others can count on you, so that when a job is given, one can depend on its being done, and done well; perseveringly, efficiently. This, I think, is important in our work, in our school work.

And the third level, which this area of responsibility covers, concerns the whole question of facing up to one's obligations, one's duties, in a manful, courageous way. Think of the tremendous effect it has, when a monk who is out with a group of boys, or on holiday, slips away to say his Office—withdraws to pray. And this is not a self-conscious act—as was that of another of our Fathers who would toss his book into the air saying: 'I must get on with the millstone.' I say this because I think younger people perhaps too easily exempt themselves from Office. I have never enquired when you take parties on outings or to camp—that kind of thing—whether it occurs to you to slip away, perhaps fifteen yards, to say a Little Hour. It has a profound effect on people! Not that this is one's motive; but it is taking one's prayer life seriously and responsibly, because this is the demand made upon us. We slip away to say Office as a mother might slip away to do the washing up.

I sense a growing unease in respect of poverty in our *Poverty . . .* Congregation and in our confederation. It is one of those difficult subjects because we are not very clear as to how, with our commitments, our work, we can really give witness to a poverty which is truly evangelical. We can sit around debating this, and talk and talk and talk. All I would urge is that we should treasure our traditional ways of expressing our poverty. We should be conscientious about asking permission for things that have been given or sent to us; or about rendering an account when we have been on a journey or on holiday—which, incidentally, I think we are good at. We should discourage gifts—especially gifts which are superfluous—without, of course, hurting potential donors. Yes, it is important not to encourage potential donors. There is nothing more horrid in the Church, I think, than the cadging priest. I do not think we have cadging priests here.

Another aspect of poverty you might remember is not forgetting to thank people when they give things, especially writing to say thank you. Saying 'Thank you' is not a conspicuously clerical virtue. It is difficult sometimes to say 'No'; but on the whole we should discourage people from giving us things. What I mean is that our style of life, our attitudes, our reactions, our values—those are all the words—have to witness to the presence of God, the presence of the Kingdom of Christ, rather than to a style of life modelled on the way in which lay people live. How difficult it is to make that sort of judgment! But let me remind you

that if you abandon—in the holidays, for instance—
clerical clothes you very quickly identify with the style
of life which prudent men, sensible men, would not
call monastic! What is meant by frugality, by simplicity
of living, is difficult to define and, naturally, with our
varied backgrounds and upbringings we have different
views. But on the whole we have been good at this.
However, it is something precious which we have to
preserve. That, Fathers, I believe, is the whole spirit
of this Chapter. We have, I think, precious values
handed on to us by our forefathers. But they have to
be preserved with care, with love, and a certain pride.
Whatever we become, whatever we do in the future,
these must be part of our monastic life. I believe that
if we become slack on any of these, we will not survive;
I would go so far as to say we do not deserve to.
But because we have these values, we shall survive.

30. 11. 71

5. Simplicity

We have, Fathers, in our Community a great deal for
which we ought daily to thank God. In our day-to-day
living we are conscious of things which do not seem
to work smoothly, and we are aware of problems
which face the Church and monastic life in our time.
But it would be foolish to fail to stand back and assess
how blessed we have been. One of the most remarkable
things that has emerged in the last few weeks has
been the evident concern of the Community for its
prayer life, whether it be over the controversy which
we have had about our liturgy, or whether it be the
interest which certain members of the Community
are taking in the contemporary movements of prayer
and the power of the Spirit. All these things are important. We should recognise, too, that the Community
is working hard and to good effect. It is not easy
to guide and educate young people today, as you
know better than I. Academically, culturally and athleti-
cally—as far as I can judge—I would think that the
school is better now than it has perhaps ever been in
the past. Our main concern is, of course, the Christian
formation of the boys, and I do not suppose that

you who are on the school staff would think that you
have yet achieved perfection in that!

We have been blessed too, I think, by the way in
which we have been able to help various groups of
people who have come here, and the generous work
done by those who involve themselves in this. And
so, as I say, if one looks at what is going on in the
Community we can say: it is strong, it is vital and
effective. There was a time when the Community—in
my monastic lifetime—was perhaps too inward-looking,
when complacency was a danger. Today, in a critical
age, we are likely to fall into the other extreme: losing
confidence; looking at what goes wrong and not building on what is going right. We recognise that under
God's providence there is much of which we can
be proud and which can make us go forward with
enthusiasm.

Monasteries in the Church today are going to be
increasingly important; of that there is no shadow of
doubt; and we have something precious to contribute.
It depends, as always, on each one of us helping everybody else to achieve the highest standards in our
devotion to God. There are three areas of our life
about which I wish to speak briefly, because they are
fundamental to our way of life as led in this monastery:
prayer, simplicity and frugality, obedience.

Prayer. Our controversy over the liturgy revealed
the precious truth that the Community is concerned
about its prayer life and thinks it very important. I
would like to say something, though, about what I
have called our 'liturgical controversy'. I did say at
the meeting that the changes which were introduced
in October were initiated by myself. I say this because
more than one person has intimated to me—some
more delicately than others—that I was, in fact, the
object or subject of a pressure group. This is untrue:
they were my ideas—bad though they seem to have
turned out—with, I think, the exception of two. I take
the responsibility for those changes, and deeply apologise to the Community for them and for the manner
in which I presented them to you. But I do not like
other people to receive the blame for things which
I have done myself. I apologise without any embarrass-
ment, because it is a good thing for Superiors to make

mistakes from time to time—and one in which this Superior is well versed! But there are irritants to be removed from the changes. You remember that I formed a group which produced a questionnaire; the answers you will find on the Calefactory table. As a result of studying them, and after discussions, the following changes seem to be required. We shall revert to the psalmody which we were using previously. We shall have Mass in choir and not go round the altar to the other side. Lauds will be after Communion.

The Crow Hotel . . .   As to simplicity and frugality. I would like to tell you a little story against myself. I think, since the Crow Hotel was reconstructed some twenty years ago, I have been there three times. Six months ago I was having lunch at this hotel—which is a very good one. At the next table was a group who spotted this cleric and wondered who he was. Could he be the Abbot of Ampleforth? They decided it could not possibly be so: an Abbot would never go to a hotel of this calibre. However, they wanted to overcome their doubts and one of them came up to me and said: 'Are you the Abbot of Ampleforth?' And then it was all very jolly. But I met later somebody who told me that Mary, or whoever it was, said she saw me but did not think it was me because an abbot, she thought, would not be in a first-class hotel! I am not ashamed to have been to the Crow; but it does make one ask what is expected of us by quite reasonable and sensible people. We can so easily in our mode of behaviour—in our attitudes, in the way we entertain or allow ourselves to be entertained, in the environment in which we move—find ourselves in a situation where reasonable people would not expect a monk to be. Simplicity and frugality do not necessarily just mean living in a room with few possessions: it is an attitude of mind, and it is easy for us to slip into 'the ways of the world'. We have to be on our guard, not just because of what people say or think (that should not be the motive), but because a monk ought to be both in his life-style and in his attitudes simple and frugal, in the right sense. Incidentally, I think the lady's attitude a mistaken one, but the general point will be clear to you.

Obedience is central to monastic life. The longer I live as a monk, the more I think it is remarkable that we should have chosen—or better, that we should have been chosen—for a life in which obedience and celibacy are values of importance. They are so contrary to what our natures seem to require for themselves; namely, a total independence in our choices, and fulfilment in the married state. They are quite remarkable things to choose, and as such are powerful signs of the Kingdom of God in our midst and of our dedication. Obedience is the outward sign of my determination to dedicate my whole life to God my Father; it is an expression of my love for Christ, my desire to follow him. It is a liberation, it is a freeing, so that I can be a true instrument of the Spirit. A study of monastic obedience compels one to admit that it has been influenced by elements which, I think, can only be judged unmonastic. The 'corpse-like' concept of obedience which curiously enough ꞏ belongs to St. Francis, is not monastic obedience; a 'militaristic' concept of obedience is not monastic; the idea of 'submission of judgment' is not monastic. It is equally true that monastic obedience can be affected by elements in contemporary spirituality which can be alien to monastic spirituality; such things as the primacy of conscience, the rôle of personal responsibility, obedience as primarily obedience to the Community, the claims of charity over-riding the demands of obedience, certain elements drawn from modern psychology. All these things can, and no doubt will, make their contribution to the evolution of the doctrine of obedience, but they should not detract from the centrality of obedience in the monastic way of life; much less should they be the occasion for self-deception, the pursuit of self-will.

It is my belief that obedience varies in different religious Orders. In some, obedience plays a lesser rôle than it does in the monastic life and there are different interpretations. Each Order has its own charism; each monastic house its own charism; and obedience has always played a central part in this house and has been, I believe, the source of considerable blessings. It needs a great deal of faith, a mature outlook, to see in human Superiors and in Community arrangements, the working out of God's providence. But unless we have that faith we cannot live as

8

genuine and, indeed, as happy monks. There is in our house a great tradition of obedience and there are today—as in the past—shining examples which are a great matter for edification. We should, each of us, encourage ourselves and others in the pursuit of obedience. Devotion to prayer, simplicity and frugality (in attitude, mind, and behaviour), and obedience— these are our heritage from the past in our monastic tradition. There are signs in our house of many blessings of God mentioned earlier on. I like to think it is because we are concerned with prayer, because we are concerned with obedience, because we are concerned with poverty, that these blessings come. From time to time we need to re-affirm our belief in these values, because for us, I think, these are the prerequisites in our search for God, in our love of God, and in our love and service of our neighbour.

15. 1. 73

PART TWO:

Life in the Spirit

V

Searching for God

1. The Desire to Pray

I WANT TO talk about prayer. We should distinguish two things: the obligation to pray and the desire to pray.

The desire for prayer is that internal attraction towards prayer. It is not a question of our attitude being 'I ought to pray', but a question of 'I want to pray'. It is true there is a midway stage where I can say, 'I want to do what I ought to do.' And this is fair and proper, but it is insufficient. There has to grow within us a desire for prayer, a nostalgia for prayer, a taste for prayer. Now because we are very busy and our minds preoccupied with many things, we have all experienced the difficulties life presents to our prayers. It is true that the work we do is done under obedience and for that fact alone has a particular value – apart, that is, from its intrinsic value. But a problem arises because it is not easy for us to maintain a state of recollection, our gaze and attention set upon the Lord. In monasteries where there is no active work of the kind in which we are engaged, this sense of the presence of God is more easily acquired at an earlier age in the monastic life. For us it is more difficult, but by no means impossible. But it does depend on our having a definite, business-like attitude towards prayer. I am not talking about private prayer or liturgical prayer specifically – I am abstracting from both and talking in general terms. But the desire for prayer is something which comes, I suspect, only slowly and with practice. I think it is a truism of prayer to say that the desire for it, the taste for it, follows from the practice of it. It is not because we are drawn to prayer that we first begin to pray; more often we have to begin prayer, and then the taste and the desire for it come. Similarly, therefore, if for one reason or another we stop praying or allow prayer to drop out of our lives, then the taste and desire go too. Anyone who has any doubt about that should reflect on the sort of things that can happen during our vacation—how easily the taste for prayer can go or become enfeebled.

A sense of unreality ... It is true that the life of prayer has its own difficulties. There can be no serious practice of prayer which is not accompanied by darkness and a sense of unreality. Indeed, the darkness and unreality are part and parcel of prayer. They are the modes whereby our faith is purified—our being deprived of the props and supports which were necessary at an earlier stage. This is a difficult and sometimes frightening experience because we have the sense that nothing is happening—a sense that prayer is a frustrating experience. As all the spiritual writers tell us, these are the dangerous moments, because it is at this point that we can be overcome by discouragement and so fail to persevere. The same can happen in regard to Divine Office. We can be discouraged by a sense of unreality—a sense of 'non-relevance' to our lives, and be tempted no longer to persevere in applying our minds, to concentrate on what we are supposed to be doing in Choir. But tenacity and perseverance are basic qualities which one must expect to find in a monk: qualities, indeed, which St. Benedict demands of the postulant who applies for admission. We must also be business-like. And again it is a matter of reflection upon the things of God, *Lectio divina*: the necessary pre-requisite for a lively and true prayer; a necessary pre-requisite for concentration on Divine Office. For that is what reflective reading, *Lectio divina*, is—not preparation for a sermon, not reading theology for its own sake, but prayerful reading which enables the Holy Spirit to move our minds towards an understanding of, an insight into, the things of God, coupled with a desire to give ourselves to God and to express this in prayer.

I remember Fr. Paul[1] saying that if you get the work of the school right, everything else follows. It is equally true that if you get the prayer of a community right, the rest follows. Prayer is the most important thing.

[2] Fr. Paul Nevill, Headmaster of Ampleforth College, 1924–54.

We can have the attitude, for instance (unconscious, I know) that we have the day to plan, all these activities in which we must engage, and then, somehow or other, prayer to be fitted in. Or we can have the attitude that we have prayers to say, and look upon the work we have to do as flowing from our prayer. And when we are truly convinced of the priority that prayer must have, of its value, then we will be anxious to give it, in practice, the primacy it deserves, not only in our individual lives, but in the life of the Community. But as monks, and monks engaged in a worthwhile work for God, either here or with our Fathers on the parishes, prayer is *the* means whereby the Spirit can guide us. When we are truly praying, then we can begin to see Christ in our neighbour; when we are really praying we can begin to live for the Father. Then our monastic life begins to be a life in and with Christ for the Father. This is what we came here for, this is the most important thing in our lives.

I have often reflected, and possibly said this previously, that there should be in every monk a potential Trappist, a potential Carthusian — or, put it this way — there should be a little regret in each one of us that God did not call us to be a Carthusian: a regret that this great vocation was not offered to us. If we have that thought within us, we will be saved from activism: we will be spared the danger of failing to see the hand of God in our lives, the hand of God in our work. It is prayer which gives spiritual insight. There is a very simple equation with which I will conclude: a man of prayer equals a man of God; and a man of God equals a man of spiritual influence.

A potential Trappist . . .

12. 5. 67

2. The Prayer of Incompetence

It is seldom one hears priests talking about prayer. They seem inhibited as they try to explain what goes on when we are praying. I think, however, that every Superior of a religious community is bound from time to time to talk about prayer. My aim is to talk in general terms to a specific group — those who have been by and large faithful to prayer over the years, yet in practice seem to meet frustration and difficulty: those who often feel they are getting nowhere.

There are two aspects in our life which militate against the practice of mental prayer or the apparent success of such prayer.

The first is our preoccupation with the many activities in which we are engaged, under obedience. Our minds can be so crowded with anxieties and cares or the difficulty of fitting so much into one day, that when we come to mental prayer our minds are not relaxed, not refreshed.

The second difficulty, which is connected with the first, is mental fatigue. It is something from which all of us in this Community suffer from time to time, and many of us for considerable periods. We have to be sure, of course, when we come to mental prayer, that we are playing our part. I am not referring to obvious things such as being faithful to the half-hour set apart for this purpose; nor to such impediments to prayer as laziness, self-seeking, and the like. One presumes that, in accordance with monastic principles, there is in our lives a general orientation towards the things of God. I am thinking of the part we play when we are actually involved in this practice which we call mental prayer. And we should not be reluctant to adopt a method when we pray. Manuals often suggest that to follow a method is something proper to the initial stages of prayer, and then, as time goes on, a method is no longer needed. This is false. It is quite wrong to think of prayer as an ascending thing. It is, in fact, the experience of most of us that it is something changing, and that often we should revert to an earlier method sooner than we do. One is reluctant to propose any specific method. Besides, were we not all brought up on the principle that the best way to pray is the way that suits you? That, indeed, is true. The prayer of two persons is never identical. What suits one will not suit another. But if we find ourselves unable to pray, in the sense that our minds wander and it is difficult to focus attention on the Lord; that nothing is happening; when this occurs, then is the time to revert to a method that has helped at an earlier stage. And in the experience of us all there are methods which do seem to have helped. For some it will be to go back to vocal prayer—that is, the use of a set formula. St. Teresa of Avila talks of the old nun who never got any further than saying the Our Father during times of mental prayer. She then adds that this nun had reached a very high stage of spirituality. But it is the initial practice of going through a formula that can be a valuable starting-point.

In times of stress or exhaustion it can help to divide the half-hour into, say, four parts: the first ten minutes spent on the Kyrie of the Mass, then a period of going through the Gloria, a third reflecting on an Offertory prayer, and the fourth perhaps reading the prayers of the Consecration. Something of the kind can be useful and helpful. We may, it is true, get no further than repeating the formulas; they may still seem meaningless, to have no message; yet the fact of keeping this up faithfully will eventually bear fruit in a way I hope to suggest in a moment.

Some prefer the use of their imagination without words; others like to be struck by ideas. But remember, word or image or idea is only a starting point; we have to go beyond these to the Person: the Person of God or one of the Persons of the Trinity. For this surely is the essence of prayer. We need to have an awareness of God and to respond to that awareness. And that response will come sometimes in words, and sometimes at a curious baffling level where there is neither word nor thought. And this is the central point of my talk.

Many of us feel, I think, and often quite early in the religious life, that methods get in the way rather than help. When I talk to experienced priests, especially those who live what we call the contemplative life, they say that their disciples abandon methods and go through what, for want of a better word, can be described as the prayer of quiet. This is a prayer in which neither words, nor ideas, nor images have meaning for us. We are simply aware of God, and our response to him finds expression in none of these ways. It is just a response from the depths of our being.

The German theologian Paul Tillich came near, I think, to describing this kind of prayer (he is quoted in *Honest to God*[1]), when he spoke of God as being the depth or 'ground' of our being. For there is, I

[1] *Honest to God*, John A. T. Robinson, S.C.M. paperback, p. 22.

believe, at an elementary level of prayer a realisation
that God is present deep within each one of us. St.
Teresa of Avila asked: 'Why do you look for God
here, why do you look there? God is within you.'

No awareness
of prayer . . .

But, dear Fathers, this is not a form of prayer with
which I am very familiar, I must confess. There is
another kind of prayer which is, I think, the prayer
of many of us. It does not follow from any method,
because method does not help. There is no awareness
of prayer. Now, that is a state on which most of us
can talk fairly eloquently. It is the 'prayer of incompetence'. And this I think is the normal experience
of many of us. A method does not help: images or
ideas seem to be obstacles, and yet when we abandon
these we find we still have no awareness of God. It
is at this point that we are tempted to give up. Again
St. Teresa warns us that people abandon prayer as
something unrewarding—as something not for them.

What is the point of this? We are meant, I think,
to learn many lessons when we are left in this state,
but there are two in particular. And the first is to
realise that in prayer it is the giving which matters
rather than the receiving; that we are going through
this exercise (it is an unfortunate word but you know
what I mean) for the sake of God first rather than
for the sake of ourselves. In other words, we are prepared to be just kneeling or sitting or walking, without
very much happening and are prepared to go on in
that state, waiting (and we may wait for years)—
waiting as one who has to grow in humility and in
the realisation of the limitations of the human soul:
that it must be God who gets into touch with us, not
vice versa. That is the first lesson to be learnt.

The second lesson is that there is no progress in
prayer without progress in faith, a purification of faith.
And this entails the removal of all the props which
depend on human endeavour, human reasoning, signs
and the rest. It is the naked faith which is a terrifying
experience and yet is the meeting point ultimately
between God and ourselves in the depth of our being.
This experience of the purification of faith is not
normally one which comes early in religious life. It
comes late.

Well, dear Fathers, these are some thoughts on

prayer. But we must remind ourselves of what we learnt as novices: that the key to the whole thing is perseverance. We must learn to wait, never to give up, to revert to simple methods and only abandon these when they are no longer of any help.

We may wonder sometimes what is the result of our fidelity to prayer. From day to day there is little result that we can see or assess. Only when one looks back over the years does one come to realise that our convictions concerning the things of God are, despite all, clearer than they were. And I think, finally, that the most important result of fidelity to prayer is that, despite everything, we want to go on praying.

3. 2. 68

3. The Depth of our Being

Last week we were talking about prayer. And if you remember, we said it would be foolish, when we find prayer difficult, to fail to revert to a method of praying, either by concentration on words, by the use of our imagination, or by dwelling on an idea. Naturally a prayer of this type would most probably be a combination of all three: an attempt to penetrate through the image, word, or idea to the person, the person of God.

I went on to say that probably in the monastic life one can move on from method, because method no longer seems to help. And then I described two states of prayer: prayer of quiet, when there is an awareness of God in the very depth of our being, a response which is not necessarily translated into words, image, or idea. But more often we find ourselves, I said, in what we term the prayer of 'incompetence', where method is useless and seems to be an obstacle and yet, at the same time, there is not an awareness of God, and a seemingly conscious response is impossible. I went on to say that this is a state in which many of us find ourselves for a considerable time. In the course of this prayer, which does not seem to be a prayer, we have to learn that prayer is essentially a giving to God as well as a receiving from him. It is also a time to learn to recognise our limitations.

I want to continue to think about this prayer of 'incompetence'. To begin, I want to make a simple statement which is very much a generalisation. Changes in one's spiritual life are, I think, closely related to the psychological changes which take place within us as time goes on. Early in the monastic life, because normally we tend to be young, our dominant characteristic is 'doing', whereas when we get older it is 'being'. That is an extreme over-simplification, but you will probably understand what I mean. Anyway, this fact has an effect upon our prayer: early on we are active and busy at prayer, whereas later we find this distasteful and so are forced back on to just 'being', and it is about this I would like to talk.

I say there are dominant characteristics in age groups. This is indeed an over-simplification, for what I have described as the prayer of 'incompetence' occurs both earlier on in life and later. I emphasise this, because one comes across people who have been in religious life say ten, fifteen or twenty years and have grown disillusioned because they have come to the conclusion that there is no progress for them in prayer, no awareness of God, nor can they stimulate in themselves any response. They feel abandoned.

There are three points I would like to make.

'Speak, Lord' . . .   First. It is important to adopt the attitude of waiting, of just being present at prayer even though the effort seems to us unrewarding. Success or failure—that is the attitude of Samuel: 'Speak, Lord, for your servant hears.'[1] This attitude may be as far as we will get. And in my opinion it is a mistake to expect in prayer a response from God. Often God's response is outside prayer. And often we do not link up an outside response with the effort we put into prayer. God speaks to us through events, through other persons, in opportunities presented to us day by day. But he speaks to us essentially and above all in the depths of our being, inspiring in us a greater wanting for God; and this, I think, is one of the characteristic fruits of the life of prayer; a greater desire for God, although our understanding of God is no greater now than it was, say, ten years ago. And then a greater understanding of the things of God will probably accompany that; though again,

[1] I Sam. 3:10.

it is not an understanding based upon theological
enquiry or on any mental activity of ours: it is a knowledge of God based on our wanting God and a conviction growing all the time, which is in fact a thing of
grace and not something of our own discovery or
contrivance. This being so common an experience in
people who at the same time complain that they are
no good at prayer, we should see, I think, that fidelity
to prayer is closely linked with things which go on
inside us and will go on in and through the events of
every day.

Secondly. It is important to accept the condition
of being apparently abandoned by God. All the spiritual
writers underline this point. And how easy it is,
when we are engaged in the prayer of incompetence,
to forget this, and how rewarding it is when we remember, finding ourselves in a mood of frustration, to
thank God that we are in this state; to recognise that
it is obviously what he thinks best for us! I find helpful
the story of the two blind men on the way to Jericho
as told in St. Matthew's Gospel. It is a wonderful
picture of what goes on so often in prayer. Our Lord
comes to them and says: 'What would you have me
do for you?' and they say: 'Lord, we would have our
eyes opened.'[1] That is the state we are in before God.
We are blind, we cannot see God with our senses,
and our deductions from what we know or are thinking
about the word of God itself—how little power they
have to bring us to God! We are blind and our eyes
need the touch of our Lord's hand to enable us at
times to see even dimly. We need to recognise that we
are blind, be happy to be blind, accept being blind.

Thirdly. The experience of prayer when there is no
awareness of God and no apparent response from
ourselves should not lead us to escape from prayer or
give it up. We must try without strain and without
being complicated, to turn our minds, as far as we can,
to God. But that is of course the whole problem: the
fact that the mind cannot focus on God. Thought
cannot contain God. But we can, perhaps, try to
dwell on some of the attributes of God—the important
ones, the obvious ones: to dwell on the thought of
God's love, to dwell on the thought of God's mercy,

[1] Matt. 20:33.

sometimes simply to repeat phrases from the Gospel;
snippets of prayer we have learnt at one time or another,
just to take our attention away from other things,
even if it cannot take us right into the presence of God.

I have talked about this prayer of 'incompetence'
because I am convinced that it is a state in which many
people find themselves; one which can depress and make
them think prayer is not for them. But it is, I suspect,
a common experience and we should accept it as a
state in which God often wishes us to be. It is a good
state and probably much better for us than prayer in
which we are aware of God's presence—whatever that
may **mean**. It is a valid state of prayer provided that
in our lives we are fulfilling our part; and in this connection it is important to be faithful to spiritual reading.
Is it not true that if our prayer is not going well, if our
taste for prayer is fading, the first thing we have to examine
is whether we are keeping up our spiritual reading?

Fathers, today people want to know about prayer.
If one goes to a Retreat or a conference it is prayer
that people want to hear about. Some priests and
monks are good at prayer, great men of prayer, who
have a deep understanding of prayer, but are not
articulate. Others, alas, are articulate, but not very
good at it. Think of the irresistible strength of those
who are good at prayer and can talk about it! Others'
needs are not, of course, a motive for our being men
of prayer, but they are a reminder of our responsibility.
We often have meetings and conferences on how to
teach religion. How often do we have conferences on
how to teach prayer? How often do we have sermons
on how to pray? But this is the great need of today,
because there is a demand for it. And this, as you know,
is the central fact of *aggiornamento*, renewal of spirit
among the people of God; and there is no renewal of
spirit where there is no responsible life of prayer.

10. 2. 68

4. Nostalgia for God

To pray is to try to make ourselves aware of God
and in that awareness respond to him. It is an attempt
to raise our minds and hearts to God.

Abbot Herbert used to tell us that to try to pray was in fact to pray.

Prayer is an act of faith, hope, and charity. It is always an act of faith: 'Lord, we would have our eyes opened.' Our Lord, let me remind you, puts to us the question he put to the two blind men on the way to Jericho: 'What would you have me do for you?' 'Lord, we would have our eyes opened.'[1] He puts to us the question he put to that other blind man whom, as St. John records, he cured: 'Do you believe?' 'I do believe, Lord,' the man answered, and falling down adored him.[2]

Prayer is an act of charity, an act of love. 'You know all things, Lord, you know that I love you.' It is an act of hope, because he puts to us the same question he put to certain of the apostles (in the sixth chapter of St. John): 'Would you, too, go away?' 'Lord, to whom would we go? Yours are the words of eternal life. We have learned to believe and are assured that you are the Christ, the son of God.'[3] We, also, are tempted to go away, turn away, and then we remember that there is none other to whom we can go to find eternal life.

Prayer is the cry of a humble man: one who recognises his inadequacy before God. 'Lord, be merciful to me a sinner.' 'It is not those who are in health who have need of the physician, but those who are sick.'[4] To pray is to acknowledge our dependence on God. And so we wonder why we should ask, when God is already aware of our needs. Because he told us himself that we should ask: 'Ask and you will receive.' Because our asking is part of the order of things that brings about the working of God's providence. And if our request is not answered, we know it is because his wishes for us will always be greater than our ambitions.

Gratitude . . .

Prayer is the cry also of someone who is grateful: an attitude not always found among religious, who have everything supplied to them, materially and spiritually.

[1] Matt. 20:33.
[2] John 9:38.
[3] John 6:67–9.
[4] Matt. 9:12.

A humble man is a grateful man. If it were our lot to suffer deprivation, as it is the lot of many in the world, then gratitude for the little things of life and the big things of God would come more readily to our lips.

Prayer is the song of one who strives to see the majesty and beauty of God; who can admire the wonders of the created universe in order to wonder at the Creator whose majesty and beauty those created things mirror. It is a song of response from one who has reflected on the greatness of God's love for him and who strives to return love for love. But in our day-to-day life it may often not be easy to react along these lines. That is why we have to treasure moments of solitude and silence, why we must strive to dwell on the things of God in our reading of the Scriptures, in our pondering on the happenings of the day, in our thinking. This is the part we have to play, recognising it is the Holy Spirit working within us—the Holy Spirit working within us to conform our minds to the mind of Christ, so that we come to think as Christ thinks, react as Christ reacts, so that we can pray to him and with him, 'Our Father who art in heaven . . .'—a hymn of praise, even as we pray day by day in this Choir, waiting for the coming of the Kingdom of God, striving to learn his will, laying before him our daily needs—the needs of our families, of those who pass through this school, of our friends, of the whole world. And we should be saddened at the thought of the inadequacy that is ours, and strive with great humility to love God more and more. Prayer is a dialogue of love between God and ourselves: it is the cry of the creature prostrate before the majesty of God.

For us poor mortals, the task of praying will not always give us day by day a rich reward. And yet fidelity to prayer will bring with it a greater regard for prayer and, please God, a greater nostalgia for God himself.

17. 2. 68

5. The Love of God

The more one thinks of the spiritual life, the more one thinks about prayer; the more one tries to find an appropriate basic attitude to the religious life, so much the more does one realise that this must be one of love. I wonder whether the thought of God as Love has been sufficiently evident in the teaching of religion to the young. There is a story about a boy who went into an apple store. His parents were out, and there was no one around; and he wanted to take an apple. Nobody, he reflected, would see him. Then he thought again: someone would see him: God would see him and God would be angry if he took an apple. If one is brought up on stories of that kind there develops deep in the unconscious a distorted view of who God is, what kind of a person he is. Our basic attitude should be the realisation that God is Love. We should ponder on the first Epistle of St. John, chapter 4.

Now, I suppose there is no human being—I certainly hope this is so—who has not had some experience of love, some feeling of affection for another. This basic experience is the one that comes nearest if we attempt to explain what it means to love God. You will remember, I am sure, those fine words of Dr. Dominian when he said: 'Human love is an instrument we can use to explore the mystery of divine love.' And it is. We know the command to love God with our whole heart and our whole soul. And yet that experience is indeed difficult to understand, to analyse, to explain. What does it mean to love God? I suggest we understand it something like this: if I have experienced love or affection for others, I can comprehend dimly, inadequately, incompletely, not so much what God should mean to me, but what I mean to God.

It is difficult to understand how the love I feel for another person will show me how to love God. Can I feel towards God as I do towards another human being? Perhaps I should: perhaps one day I shall. Few of us, I suspect, can say that this is how it is. The key that unlocks the mystery of God's love is something as follows. When I experience love, either in giving it to another or in receiving it, then I begin to see what I mean to God. I love a particular person very much, and that person means much to me. Now I understand what I mean to God. We only love God, St. John tells us, because God first loved us.

Psychologically this seems the right way round. Our

The mystery of God's love . . .

attitude towards others often changes because we have discovered their attitude towards us. Perhaps we disliked someone, were suspicious, and then one day discovered that he likes us, admires us. Our attitude changes: we warm to him.

And so it is in the spiritual life. Our response, our attitude, depends on our realisation of God's attitude towards us. If I experience love or have experienced it, this is the means whereby I can explore the mystery of God's love. Not that I must have a love for God similar to that which I experience for others, but experience itself shows me what I mean to God. And the fact of living in that thought, dwelling in that thought, will reveal secrets and increase in us the realisation of the depth, strength, and warmth of his love. Inevitably, as in all the most important human concerns, there are dangers and pitfalls: the more precious something is, the more fragile it tends to be, the more in need of protection.

There is, for instance, a danger of being in love with love—that is, with the idea of love—to the extent of making God an impersonal object of love or someone we know about already. Instead, through a willingness to surrender ourselves, we should discover that we can know and relate to the inner nature of God as a person.

We must try to understand God through the truth revealed to us by the Word made flesh. We must try to interpret authentically the good news contained in the Gospel according to St. John. That, I think, is what some of the saints were trying to do when they said that it is more important to love God than to know him. From this can be developed the theme of the prayer of desire which for many of us is, I think, at different times in our monastic life, the only prayer of which we are capable—that simple longing to respond to a love which, we have learned, was first given to us.

17. 11. 70

VI

'*Christ became for us obedient unto Death*'

1. Looking forward to the joy of Easter

ST. BENEDICT IN one phrase—'looking forward to the joy of Easter'[1]—sets the whole tone to our Lenten observances. We are to look forward to the joy of Easter, to the joy of sharing in the life of the Resurrection. By baptism we have passed from death to life; we have passed from separation from God to union with him through grace; by baptism we were incorporated into the Passion, Death, and Resurrection of our Lord. The Christian life is lived with the life of Christ in the soul. It should be leading to peace and to joy. But in our experience it does not always work out like that. The full effect of the Resurrection of Christ will only act upon us when we come to the Beatific Vision: only then will joy and peace be complete—unable to be taken away from us. Now we live in expectation of this: no longer condemned to separation from God though not yet united in the way he has prepared; for we are not yet, as St. Thomas says, *in patria*, in our homeland, but *in via*, on the way,—and often a *via dolorosa*, a painful way. And so we should see Lent as a 'sharing' in the Passion of Christ. St. Benedict tells us that our lives should be Lenten in character, always; but because we are not strong enough for that, in these days at least let us make a special effort. Let us remind ourselves that if we are to be our Lord's disciples we must take up his Cross and follow him.

There are, in life as we lead it, abundant opportunities for meeting the Cross: daily opportunities. If we are frustrated by too much to do, the failure of others to

[1] Rule, chapter 49.

131

implement our ideas, to appreciate our difficulties; if we see things going wrong—all these can be sources of annoyance. But at the same time they are golden opportunities, if we accept them joyfully. This does not mean we have to be stoical. It does not mean we no longer strive to improve things, to remove blatant contradictions, and so forth. But remember, when things are not going well, the process of putting them right lies in the future: it is a task to do later on. It is the present moment that matters in the spiritual life, because the present moment is the only one that exists. Even though you find yourself in an intolerable position, one in which you think you have no right to be, accept it here and now as the Cross; then later you can plan how to do better. There is no contradiction between accepting here and now some difficulty and later, on a future occasion, striving to remove it. But never miss the opportunity of the present difficulty, the present moment.

The dark night . . .   Many of us have to suffer, perhaps for quite a long time, what spiritual books call 'the dark night of the soul'. It is a bit embarrassing to apply to ourselves these rather high-sounding experiences, but they do happen to us: people undergo long periods in their monastic life when things do not seem to make sense; when God seems to be remote; when prayer seems to be almost impossible; when Office is scarcely tolerable. These things do happen. Accept them whole-heartedly as part of the *via dolorosa*. The saints who learnt this —that is, to accept God's will for them in the form of the Cross if that is what he chooses—discovered a peace and a joy which surpasses our understanding. Perhaps not many of us here have met that, but we know enough about the lives of the saints to have discovered that there is something towards which we can strive and which St. Benedict talks about in the Prologue to his Rule.

We have, it is true, the life of the Resurrection in our souls, but for us who are still *in via*, the Resurrection has to be lived in the context of the Passion. Now, just as voluntary prayer gives meaning to the daily round of obligatory prayer, so it is true that voluntary penance makes us more aware of the rôle of involuntary penance in our spiritual lives. It is the practice of giving up this or taking on that which trains our minds to see the Cross when it is at hand unchosen and unbidden. It is axiomatic that the Cross we get is the one we most dislike: we would choose any other. But it is equally true that the Cross which is ours is the one Christ wants us to bear.

And so, Fathers, it is with such thoughts as these that we would do well to embark on this Lent – cheerfully, joyfully, because the Lord delights in a joyful giver.

3. 3. 65

2. Correcting weaknesses

We are a bit late in reading the Rule of St. Benedict about Lent – in turning our minds to this particular period in the liturgical year. You will recall some of the phrases of the Rule: It is to be a period when we lead lives of greater purity; when we expiate our negligences; when we refrain from sin, and apply ourselves to prayer with tears, reading, compunction of heart, abstinence. Let us look at some of these phrases and consider their relevance at the present time.

It is good for us to recognise that we are negligent, that we have to expiate the negligences of other times. It is good, I think, to confess and acknowledge our weakness and insufficiencies, our inadequacies in our service of God. There will be no occasion when that will not be an appropriate gesture. As we advance in our monastic lives I am certain that this coming to terms with our inadequacy is, in fact, not something which leads to despondency: on the contrary it can lead to great peace. We should reflect once again on the parable in St. Luke's Gospel: the story of the Pharisee and the publican; and our Lord's words at the calling of Levi: 'It is not those who are in health . . .'[1] These are some of the great truths of the Gospel which are a constant source of consolation. In fact, one can say that the more we realise our shortcomings, the greater is our claim on the mercy and goodness of God – and that is a source of immense peace. But it

[1] Matt. 9:12.

must not be, and is not, a charter for complacency.
St. Benedict tells us that in Lent we have to 'apply'
ourselves: which in simple terms means, not so much
to do extraordinary things, but to concentrate on
getting ordinary things right. We have to try to be
better monks, and this will include being better Christians and, indeed, better human beings.

Loving our neigh-bour ...
An area where we can usefully examine ourselves
and make a special effort to rectify what is wrong, is
that of relationships with one another in community
life. I think we have always considered that our Community life here is a strong one and that we get on, by
and large, extremely well with one another. That is
certainly true; but there is no room for complacency.
On the contrary, this is something we must watch
carefully, something precious which we must treasure.
We ought to consider whether we treat each other
with the courtesy, civility, sensitivity, generosity and
understanding that are necessary; to ask, also, whether
the needs of others are more important to us than our
own; to reflect how generously or how selfishly we
lead our community life. Everyone in the Community
should feel acceptable and accepted. Each must be in
some measure the object of my concern, my interest,
my compassion. This is a time when we should concentrate on the rôle we play within the Community
life. If we find ourselves not talking to certain people,
we should scrutinise the reasons why: whether it is
because we find them boring, or because we do not
agree with them, or even perhaps because we are
frightened of them. Not to converse with people
because we are slightly frightened of them is also a
fault. We have to make an effort with everyone. Why?
Because that is the right thing for a human being to
do—still more so for Christians, because Christ lives
in each one of us. To neglect anyone in the Community
is to neglect Christ; to fail to treat anyone with courtesy
or civility is to fail to treat Christ in that way. If what
I say is not true, how are we to interpret the passage
in the Gospel where we are told to feed the hungry,
clothe the naked?

It is easy to look afield to exercise charity—our
service to Christ—yet to neglect the Father or Brother
next to us in the Choir or the refectory. Concern and

compassion, interest and understanding, are crucial in
our monastic and Christian living. We have always
had, I think, in this Community a strong sense of
family pride, of loyalty to each other. Again, I think
we should examine ourselves as to how strong that
pride belongs to us individually, how loyal we are to
each other. This concerns our relationship with outsiders. It is easy to criticise to an outsider some member
of the Community. What is our motive when we
criticise one of our brethren or belittle him? I emphasise
this, not because I have heard or detected anything
that could suggest our charity is weakening, but because
it is important from time to time to remind ourselves
of such things. After all, love of our neighbour is the
test of our love of God.

In this season we must face up to our attitude to *Do we want*
God. Are we truly seeking him? Do we want to do *what he*
his will? Do we accept his will as translated to us in *wants? . .*
the circumstances of our living? Do we see his will
in the things that happen to us—the difficulties, the
frustrations, the hundred-and-one things that occur
each day? Do we want what he wants? Do we really
want God's will in God's way, or are we seeking God's
will in our way? This, I think, is what St. Benedict
means when he urges us in Lent to strive for 'purity
of heart': to be single-minded in our search for God—
the true end of all our actions, all our thinking, all
our prayer. And we know from experience that it is
in applying ourselves, as St. Benedict urges us, to
prayer and reading that this is most effectively obtained.
Now, we all know that in any religious life and in the
life of any priest, the two practices that tend first to
be 'dropped' are reading and prayer. Yet we know—if
we make the enormous effort needed to give a few
extra moments to prayer—that results can be out of
all proportion to the effort made. It is not necessarily
the doing of anything very great or particularly exacting that counts, but the seizing of small opportunities
—these make the difference to our attention and our
enthusiasm.

Lent is a time to give to prayer and spiritual reading
the priority they should have. It is tedious, of course,
to listen to counsels of this kind. We feel we have not
the time, and, if we have the time, we haven't the

energy. Yet it is the old story: the busiest persons are
often the most prayerful.

A word of
warning . . . It is easy, especially in the morning, to get into the
habit of being half-asleep, mooning, kidding oneself
that one is in a state of prayer. The only thing to do
is to pull oneself together and go back to a very simple
form of planned prayer. Within that context I think
the grace of God operates. It is, of course, a personal
matter, and in our Community the tradition is to leave
it to the individual.

Another thing, dear Fathers, and especially dear
Brothers. And this you should discuss with people
experienced in prayer. The entire rôle of the spiritual
guide is going out because people no longer go to
confession regularly. This is a pity; we all need to
submit our manner of prayer to a prudent Father who
can judge whether a particular type of prayer is suited
to us—whether in fact it is true prayer.

In St. Benedict, as I have emphasised, the word 'joy'
is used and that, as in everything else, should characterise our observance of Lent. We are to offer God
something of our own free will 'in the joy of the Holy
Spirit' and we are to 'look forward with the joy of
spiritual longing to the holy feast of Easter'. These
things required of us, let us carry out calmly and cheerfully, because each of us has but one ambition: to be a
dedicated servant of God, a true monk—and to be a
true monk is to be a joyful one.

12. 3. 74

3. Destined for Death

There is something chilling, austere, about the thought
of Lent: the same kind of feeling I get when I go into
a graveyard.

I recall the words of Ash Wednesday: 'Remember
man, that you are dust and to dust you will return.'
Musing on this, I thought about the connection between
death and Lent. 'Death', the late Professor Zaehner
wrote, 'is God's gift to man, a gift we should accept,
not in fear and trembling, but in joy, for we have
the assurance, not only in Christianity but in all great
religions, that what we call death is nothing worse

than the break-up of the husk of self-love and the release within us of the sap of a selfless love which is both human and divine, the Holy Spirit who dwells in the hearts of all.' I like the words, 'Death is God's gift to man, a gift we should accept not in fear and trembling but with joy.' The observances we take on in Lent can be called 'daily deaths' and life is full of 'little deaths'. Our Master told us that we could only be his disciples if we took up our Cross, and the Cross leads to death.

But it is good to realise that the 'little deaths' of each day 'release within us', in the words of Professor Zaehner, 'the sap of a selfless love . . . the Holy Spirit'. This is why Lent is important. The opening ceremony reminds us, with a realism characteristic of the Church, that we are dust and into dust we shall return. We are destined for death. But this death, this gift from God that will ultimately come to us, is the gateway to a life which is a releasing of the human and divine life in our hearts, the outpouring of the Holy Spirit. This is the mystery of Christ's death, a gift from his Father, accepted, as we know, with pain and conflict: 'Father, if it be your will, let this chalice pass from me, but not my will but yours.' It was a gift accepted with joy. The negative, the sad, the difficult, are not values in themselves, but means which lead to joy, life, and union in Christ.

St. Paul, as I have reminded you, says: 'God loves a cheerful giver.' So we must look at these 'daily deaths' and accept them with courage and joy. The penances we take on voluntary we should take on with joy because they bring us close to Christ and prepare us to celebrate the great mysteries of Christ's Death and Resurrection. This, we recall, is underlined by St. Benedict. Throughout Lent we keep our eyes on those great days, the last days of Holy Week. We prepare for them, not only because we are preparing to involve ourselves more closely in the mystery of Christ's Death and Resurrection as we celebrate it liturgically, but because death is a reality which each one of us must face. But those ashes will live again.

Those ashes will live . . .

I would urge all who have a hand in the preparation of Holy Week to plan early so that we can celebrate these days with seemliness and recollection. Our services, dear Fathers, must be done with the dignity and sensitivity to which the liturgy is entitled. We need this in our lives to raise us above ourselves, to get a glimpse of the dignity and beauty which is God. We should make a special effort in this Lenten period to improve our public prayer. Readings should be well prepared and well read. There should be nothing slipshod, nothing slovenly.

11. 2. 75

4. Crisis

I have to give you, I am afraid Fathers, bad news and probably the Community a bit of a shock.

This is a source of great sadness to me and no doubt to you. You will not expect me to tell you the reasons which led to the decision of this particular Brother to leave us. I can best sum it up, I think, by saying that the heart had gone out of his vocation. And once that happens and a man becomes unsettled to the degree where the strain is too much, it seems only prudent to release him.

No room for com- placency . . . I want, however, to talk on this subject in general for a few moments. I am not proposing to give an analysis of all the reasons which lead people to have second thoughts in our present age. Perhaps it is some consolation to know that our record is comparatively good. But that is cold comfort. I think the uncertainty of the times is one reason. I think, too, that to some extent those of us who have been brought up in the Welfare State are less easily able to take the contradictions and difficulties that are inevitable in monastic life. This is what people are finding in general. So it should not come as a surprise if we are experiencing the same kind of thing here. Whatever the cause, it calls for a great deal of heart-searching on the part of us all: there is no room for complacency; no reason to think that we, here, have all the answers.

On the other hand, there is no reason for loss of confidence in ourselves, in our way of life. But my experience in talking to other religious, both in other Orders and in our own, is that there is a certain failure on the part of young monks and other young religious to appreciate the gravity of the step they take when they make their Solemn Profession (even, indeed, when they make their temporary vows), a failure to understand that the decision is final and irrevocable; as final and irrevocable as the step taken by a man who enters into matrimony—if a man who gets married discovers difficulties in his life, there is no escape from the bond. There is a failure, too, to make an adult decision, which has to be calculated and certain. I say this so that those who have not yet taken the final step may make certain, without becoming anxious or excited or getting the thing exaggerated in their minds, that their decision is a prudent one.

Yet, dear Fathers, you know very well you don't enter into marriage simply weighing the pros and cons. You are carried on by something else—by love. And it is because you want to serve God, because you want to love him, that you are prepared to take this step. So I don't want to give you the idea that it is only a cold, calculated step, carefully weighed, taken without warmth or enthusiasm. Of course not. It is the warmth and enthusiasm that carry you through. But at the same time you have to keep an eye on the brute fact of its being a final and irrevocable step. It is not a final step in another sense: it is the first step. It is the first step in a life lived for God without end: the beginning of something which finds its consummation, its fulfilment, in eternity. But, '*C'est le premier pas qui coûte.*'

I think, too, that people fail to understand the part which difficulties play in the religious life. When difficulties come then a crisis occurs, and when the crisis occurs there is often an inability to sustain or live through this. Now I know that talking about difficulties in monastic life is something many of us find unpalatable; perhaps the theme has been a bit overplayed: we prefer to have words of joy, words of encouragement. Well, that is natural. We need to dwell on the joys of our lives—we need encouragement to keep us going. Nevertheless, we must be clear about the difficulties inherent in the religious life. It is easy to have a false notion as to what Christian joy is: to think that the moment one enters the monastic life the rest is smooth-going; that sacramental grace brings with it spontaneous joy, and so forth. There can be a lot of deception in this.

I would like to touch upon two important processes in the spiritual life.

The first is the need to become less and less ego-centric and more and more God-centred. The more we learn of our own lives in a monastery and see of others' lives, the more we appreciate the importance of becoming increasingly selfless. The instinct in each of us is to want the incense to be offered to 'self': it is not instinctive to kneel down and offer it to God. The latter act would have been instinctive to unfallen human nature; but ours is a fallen nature and our instinct to draw things to self—a terrifying thought, a frightening discovery. And even when we think we are becoming increasingly spiritual, we discover how much self there is in all this. And becoming God-centred entails suffering: there is no other way. It is going to be painful. That is why I believe in the arrangements we have here for the development of the spiritual life, because in the conflicts of day-to-day living we are presented with many opportunities of dying to self and rising with Christ. This dying and rising is fundamental to the spiritual life. It is a truth we ignore at our peril.

Knowledge through faith . . .

Secondly, I would remind you that there is no progress in charity without purification of faith. This is exemplified in our Blessed Lady. She was often baffled. She did not understand. She 'kept these things in her heart'.[1] Read those texts closely and you will see what I mean. Faith must be purified. Those many props which seem important must, in a truly spiritual life, be removed—so that there is no prop left, only God. This is very hard. But we know it is so, from our reading, in the spiritual writers, of the aridities in prayer; the difficulties in understanding the things of God. After all, we have given our lives to God and yet, so often, he seems elusive. We long for light and are left in darkness. We long for consolation and find only pain. And faith is sorely tried, because faith ultimately is dependence on and acceptance of God alone. There is great talk today of insights into this truth and that, of this way of doing things and that. It is admirable: we should play a part. And yet for the individual it is a waste of time unless he grows all

[1] Luke 2:51.

the time in that knowledge of God which spiritual writers call 'experiential'—I mean the knowledge which comes through faith: that knowledge about which St. Thomas talks in his first question in the *Summa*: a knowledge which comes through prayer; an understanding which comes through prayer; a spiritual wisdom which in theological terms is 'the gift of the Holy Spirit'. But it is that knowledge of 'quasi experience' which is the one that comes through faith being purified; becoming less and less dependent on human reason, understanding, argumentation, and more and more on what God will reveal in the depths of a man's soul, just when the soul seems to be shrivelled.

Dear Fathers, I have only told you what you will find in any spiritual book; what you will find in reading the mystics. In the ordinary course of events such experiences are bound to be ours, to a greater degree or a less—this aridity and dryness, these 'difficulties of the monastic life'. Such 'difficulties' often suggest getting up in the morning, obedience, and so on. But one comes up against the sudden, supreme difficulty of wanting God with all one's soul and not finding him. This can be saddening, frightening. It can make us want to turn back. The fatal thing to do is to turn back. When this experience comes, you need to be generous and courageous. You also need to be open: to seek advice, seek help. The ways of God are not learnt primarily from books. The wisdom of God comes through people, those who have lived it, experienced it. Your ears should be sensitive to the advice you will get from persons whom you suppose have not had these experiences—in fact, they have, each in his own way. And so do not be tempted to run away. Rejoice, because these things are not obstacles: they are opportunities. It is better to walk through darkness, the Lord guiding you, than to sit enthroned in light that radiates from yourself.

23. 6. 65

5. Penetrating the secret

We are going to think and pray about the happenings during the last few days of our Lord's life: his passage, his *transitus* from this world to his place in majesty at the right hand of his Father. The Church associates herself with these events because the history of the Mystical Body and of its members is conformed to the pattern of our Lord's life. Whenever we celebrate the mysteries of Christ—the liturgy—we have to try, as St. Paul says, to penetrate the secret revealed to us by God the Father, and by Jesus Christ in whom is stored the whole treasury of wisdom and knowledge. We live these mysteries in the liturgy so as to grow in our understanding of the mysteries of Christ and translate these into our lives. So our task is to penetrate the 'secret revealed to us by God the Father and Jesus Christ'.

I would like to say a word about the part the Cross plays in our lives. I said recently, if you remember, that if we are to be followers of Christ we have to take up our Cross daily and follow him. It is not for us to claim to sit on the right hand or the left of the Father, unless we have first drunk of the chalice. It is remarkable that in the Gospel, as far as I remember, our Lord does not talk about following him or being his disciples without a reference to the Cross or to the chalice, the symbol of suffering.

In our daily lives there are many opportunities for carrying the Cross—not least misunderstandings, an unearned rebuke, gnawing anxiety, ill-health, fatigue. Now we have to decide whether these are obstacles to happiness or a path leading to it.

Nobody can love suffering, but we can love to suffer. The two are entirely different. Instinctively we recoil from suffering, but we can learn to suffer for a positive dynamic reason. After all, our Lord in the garden of Gethsemane recoiled from the Passion, but accepted it willingly—more than that, lovingly. Now in this matter of carrying the Cross it is not the negative aspect which counts: it is the positive—the good which it causes, the good to which it leads. The Cross on its own does not make sense. The Cross together with the Resurrection does. Putting off, as St. Paul says, the old self and the habits that go with it is not enough. We have to be clothed in the new self.

Clothed in the new self... 'If true knowledge', St. Paul writes, 'is to be found in Jesus, you will have learnt in his school that you must be quit now of that old self, whose way of life you remember; the self that wasted its aims on false dreams. There must be a renewal in the inner life of your minds; you must be clothed in a new self created in God's image, justified and sanctified through the truth.'[1]

Those difficulties of every kind which I mentioned, we have to see as opportunities to be 'quit of the old self'; as opportunities of growth in the image of Christ, that we may become more Christ-like, share more fully in his life, be possessed by the Spirit. This is St. Benedict's point in his chapter on humility:

'When all these degrees of humility have been climbed, the monk will presently come to that perfect love of God which casts out all fear; whereby he will begin to observe without labour, as though naturally and by habit, all those precepts which formerly he did not observe without fear; he will be motivated no longer by fear of hell, but by love of Christ, through good habit and delight in virtue. And this will the Lord deign to show forth by the power of his Spirit in his workman now cleansed from vice and from sin.'[2]

It is my conviction that each day in our monastic life we are given opportunities of growing in humility.

It is a fundamental virtue, and painful to acquire. But everyone recognises a humble man. And everyone loves a humble man. I have often reflected that if I have a duty to love my neighbour, I have a duty to make myself lovable in proportion as I am humble. I have another thought too: why is it that one likes rogues? I think it is because rogues cannot be proud, and so there is something likeable about them. Nobody dislikes a genuinely humble person, and we have a duty to be lovable, therefore a duty to be humble.

We can welcome the Cross as a way of experiencing the kind of suffering our Lord experienced. We talk glibly about the Passion and suffering of our Lord, in a general kind of way without pausing to imagine what they were like. I think often of the disappointment

[1] Eph. 4:21.
[2] Rule, chapter 7.

and sadness of our Lord when, early in his ministry, his own kinsmen, his own friends at Nazareth, wanted to throw him down from the cliff. Let us reflect on his being rejected by his own people, deserted by his friends; the desolation in the garden, the abandonment on the Cross—apart from physical torment. And yet, as I have said previously, we learn the secret of the Resurrection when we learn the secret of the Cross. And it is when we are called to share in some way in the suffering of Christ that we come to understand not only what he experienced but what this was leading to. For every cross leads to resurrection. I like to think of life as each day being prepared by God's providence, and it is in many ways the road to the Cross. But it leads to a greater understanding of our Lord, a greater sharing in his Resurrection.

The secret of the Resurrection . . .

Each day should see me more humble; each day more willing to accept what comes my way. Thus I become more closely united to the Lord—grow, as I grow in grace, in the love of his Father.

Let us consider the value of the Cross in the Church, pondering the words of St. Paul: 'I am glad of my sufferings on your behalf, as in this mortal frame of mine I help to pay off the debt which the afflictions of Christ still leave to be paid, for the sake of his body, the Church.'[1] Words difficult to understand, but of enormous consolation: when the Cross weighs heavily this is contributing to the whole life of the Church. The Cross is not something to make us less human. No, it leads us in Christ and with Christ to the Father. This is the Gospel. This is St. Paul: 'I share in the Passion of Christ, to share in his Resurrection.'[2] And again: 'Risen with Christ you must lift your thoughts above, where Christ now sits at the right hand of God. You must be heavenly-minded, not earthly-minded. You have undergone death, and your life is now hidden with Christ in God. Christ is your life and when he is made manifest, you too will be made manifest in glory with him.'[3]

4. 4. 66

[1] Col. 1:24.
[2] Rom. 6:5.
[3] Col. 3:1–4.

6. The Golden moments

No one can accuse St. Paul of being a pessimist; for him life was cheerful, rewarding, fulfilling. His doctrine is one of hope. But the passage of his upon which I would like to meditate is in his Second Epistle to the Corinthians: 'More than ever I delight to boast of the weaknesses that humiliate me so that the strength of Christ may enshrine itself in me. I am content with these humiliations of mine, the insults, the hardships, the persecutions, the times of difficulty which I undergo for Christ. When I am weakest then I am strongest of all.'[1]

Those of us who have experience of pastoral work come to realise that there are daily difficulties which cumulatively can amount to an extremely heavy burden. One can say further that in every human life there is a sadness or difficulty from which the person would gladly be free. There are, too, considerable crises of one kind or another. We call these 'crosses' and know from the Scriptures that carrying the Cross is a condition of discipleship. We know, too, that 'the grain of wheat must die . . .' We are familiar with the concept that a burden, carried as a cross, can become light. Many, however, do not derive this consolation—they become overwhelmed.

What is the rôle of the Cross in the spiritual and monastic life? Constantly God allows us to be buffeted by events and persons. There are frustrations: 'If only it had worked out as I had planned!'; failures: 'I made a fool of myself'; feelings of inadequacy: 'Others do things so much better'; misunderstandings: 'I did not mean to upset him'; being unappreciated: 'No one knows the trouble I went to.' Or we feel simply the effects of overwork and tiredness. Then there are trials unknown to others—chastity perhaps, or the trials (there are also the joys) arising from personal relationships. Today trials of faith can be burdensome. Those of us in middle-age have had to make considerable adjustments to apparent changes, even at doctrinal level. Sometimes it is just that God seems very remote —and that can be a great burden. In the process of

[1] 2 Cor. 12:9–10.

growing older and by the application of common sense we learn to adjust to situations, and learn to take to ourselves advice we know we ought to give – and would give – to others. We learn to cope with problems and to become less vulnerable.

Flashes of enlighten- ment . . .

However, we should go further, and in suffering see flashes of enlightenment and growth in our life hidden with Christ. We should recognise 'golden moments': 'when I am weakest, then I am strongest': We can come to find content, even delight, in humilia- tions, insults, hardships, persecutions, difficulties, undergone for Christ.

We become content when we realise that God is allowing us to experience – with and in his Son – some- thing of what Christ endured in Gethsemane or even in his dereliction on the Cross. There is no greater pain than the sense of having been abandoned by God: the sense that behind it all there is, after all, nothing. Ours should be at such a time the reaction of a lover to the beloved: the longing to be united to him or to her. I may not feel, it is true, that I have a love for Christ that makes me long for such an experience. But is it not true that when we find ourselves with another at a time of crisis, it is precisely in this kind of situation that we get to know the other, grow to appreciate the other and, as a consequence of that knowledge and appreciation, come to love him or love her? And so we should practise, when moments of affliction come, the art of accepting whole-heartedly and sincerely, even when our whole nature is in revolt, the Cross God has laid upon our shoulders. There is peace to be gained by thanking God for allowing us to undergo a trial. That is good doctrine: it is also good sense. Although we adjust to these situations through the ordinary process of growing old, yet it is a pity not to strike deeper, seize these opportunities for sharing in the Passion of Christ. Through sharing in his Passion we share in his Resurrection. With St. Paul let us delight to boast of our weaknesses so that, by reason of these very weaknesses, the strength of Christ may enshrine itself within us. 'The weakness of man', St. Francis de Sales said, 'is the throne of God's mercy.' The more we are conscious of our weakness, the more we become the object of God's mercy, the more we realise we are in debt, the more God will enrich us.

Another aspect: the obstacle of self-sufficiency we can raise between ourselves and God. Our failures, frustrations, and all the rest can serve to break down our egoism, our self-centredness, our self-sufficiency. The process is painful, but afterwards we give thanks to God. Then comes peace, serenity, strength. Fr. Eugene Boylan, O.C.S.O., has written in *The Virtue of Humility*, from *The Priest's Way to God*:

He has chosen us to be his friends quite gratuitously. It is not for any goodness or value he has chosen us. His motive is rather to give than to receive . . . even in human friendships, where one has chosen gratuitously and longs to do everything for the person one has chosen, what can cause so much pain and anguish as self-sufficiency? And in divine friendship the same is true. Our Lord knows our weakness, he knows our meanness, he knows our treachery, he knows our infidelity. All these he can heal and pardon. But self-sufficiency shuts the door on all his advances. He stands at the gate and knocks, and the self-sufficient will not open to him. Love calls for dependence, divine love especially so. Love wants to give, divine love most of all; but nothing can be given to the self-sufficient.

If a priest, then, asks what he is to do to meet the demands of our Lord for his friendship, the best answer is that he should imitate St. Paul and glory gladly in his infirmities that the power of Christ may dwell in him. Fr. Clerissac, O.P., said: '. . . it is our emptiness and thirst that God needs, not our plenitude.' The realisation of this truth is a great grace from God . . . human reason and human experience may perhaps indicate to us the poverty of our resources, but unless God gives us the grace, we are not likely to relish our poverty and glory in our infirmities. Yet they are the most valuable titles to divine union. 'Blessed are the poor in spirit; for theirs is the kingdom of heaven.'

11. 11. 69

7. The glory of the Suffering Servant

I have wondered often whether Peter, James, and John, when they saw our Lord transfigured, connected that event with the prophecy in the Book of Daniel concerning the coming of the Son of Man on the cloud. There is no indication that they did: it is only speculative. It was an event which impressed itself on those three apostles, although subsequently they seem to have forgotten it. 'Lord, it is well that we should be here; if it pleases you, let us make three arbours in this place, one for you, one for Moses and one for Elias.' This comes in St. Matthew's Gospel (chapter 17), and at the end of the chapter we read that while they were still together in Galilee Jesus told them: 'The Son of Man is to be given up into the hands of men; they will put him to death and he will rise again on the third day.' It goes on: 'They were overcome with fear.'

Clearly there is no reason to suppose that this particular incident was chronologically near the one described at the beginning of the chapter. But one wonders whether the primitive teaching, of which this Gospel is clearly a record, did not deliberately juxtapose these two texts and thereby show that the person of whom the book of Daniel was speaking, the Son of Man, and the person spoken of in the last part of the book of Isaiah—the Suffering Servant—are one and the same. The Son of Man, the text tells us, is to be given up into the hands of men and he will be put to death. Our Lord often tried to correct any false impression which his listeners might have as to the kind of person the Messiah was to be. His mission was to be fulfilled as indicated by the Suffering Servant of Yahweh. St. Mark refers to this twice. On the second occasion, in the eighth chapter of his Gospel, Peter, we are told, drew our Lord aside and fell to reproaching him. Our Lord rebuked him: 'Away, Satan, these thoughts of yours are man's, not God's.' Any suggestion that the rôle of Messiah was to be that of a triumphant Son of Man as portrayed in the Book of Daniel was incorrect: his mission would be fulfilled in the person of the Suffering Servant.

We ourselves should ponder on these texts during

this season of Lent as instinctively and rightly we look forward to the reign of the Son of Man. Our Christian faith has as one of its components this hope, this looking forward, this expectation of the triumph of the Son of Man in which we share and at some future time will share more fully. That is why we are more at ease in the situation in which Peter, James, and John found themselves at the Transfiguration: 'Lord, it is well that we be here.' To be involved in the situation of Yahweh's Suffering Servant is more difficult because we recoil, rightly and naturally, from the Cross. There is a danger of constructing a spirituality which will not face up to the Cross as a predominant element. Some spiritual writers today seem to forget that our Lord said: '. . . let him take up his Cross and follow me.' We shrink from the Cross because it is the natural — almost the right thing to do. Like the apostles, we are overcome with fear. It is right that we should work to rid ourselves of those things which we call the 'Cross', whether personal problems or day-to-day practical difficulties. But we need to remind ourselves again and again that the Cross is, and must be, an element in a life in which we truly follow Christ. And it is only in the intimacy of private prayer that we will do this, and learn to do it. When the burden is upon us — either the burden we carry constantly, we who are the 'wounded' products of our past or of a burden imposed upon us by the necessities of life — we must accept it in our prayer, not necessarily using words, not necessarily using thoughts, but deep within us in the presence of Christ. The wish that should constantly be ours is to share in whatever Christ wants of us; to *To fear* fear nothing; to be detached as far as we can; to prefer *nothing . . .* nothing, as St. Benedict says, to the love of Christ and therefore to want nothing other than what he wants us to accept and endure for his sake; to be firmly convinced that if we can learn to do this we will attain a true understanding of Christ's mission to the world, and ourselves share in his redeeming work. Only through following him as Redeemer shall we be able to share in his Resurrection and, ultimately, in that glory of his when he, the Son of Man, will appear on the last day.

2. 3. 71

8. Four Lenten Sermons

'I have come to call sinners, not the just'[1]

There was once a man who was a mixture of good and bad, like so many of us, plying a trade which was notoriously dishonest, a man with generous instincts, able to respond to a call on his generosity. He was a tax gatherer. In those days tax gatherers had a bad reputation; so much so that when people spoke of one they inevitably added the word 'sinner'. 'Publicans and sinners' — that's what they were called. They worked for a foreign power. Palestine at this period had been overrun by Rome and its proud people had become slaves to a foreign dominion.

Decent people did not mix with tax gatherers. They despised them. Indeed everything we know about this particular man shows him as unlikely to be chosen as an apostle. And yet he was called, and responded generously to the invitation our Lord extended to him.

Being a simple man he decided to celebrate the event. So what did he do? He called together his friends: tax gatherers too, and, in the eyes of decent people, sinners. And there they were, and in the midst of them our Lord. The decent people spotted this and began to whisper, as people often do when they believe in their own righteousness. Our Lord heard them, and in one of the most golden sentences in the whole Bible said: 'It is not those who are in health who have need of the physician, it is those who are sick. I have come to call sinners, not the just.'

St. Matthew did not know that our Lord was God. From what he had heard, and no doubt from what he had seen, he knew he must have been sent by God. For after all, Matthew was a Jew and the Jews were sensitive to their history. He knew that time and time again God had intervened to save them from domination by a foreign power. Every Jew knew that the word 'God' and the word 'Saviour' were synonymous. God saved. And he saved because he loved. Every page of the Bible reveals that. God wants to save. Every

[1] Matt. 9:12.

page of the Bible also reveals the folly of those who, by their actions, prove how much they need to be saved. There was one event which St. Matthew and every Jew knew as the most decisive in their history: it had happened 1,250 years before our Lord came. Matthew knew that his forefathers in Egypt had been subjected to slavery, their religion brought into contempt, their labour exploited; he knew that God had sent a man, a great man, Moses, and with what difficulty Moses had saved their forefathers from slavery. He knew how God had allowed one calamity after another to befall these people . . . He knew too about that solemn agreement made on Mount Sinai with the people, represented by Moses, who had spent several days on that mountain alone with God. He knew that at that time this nomad tribe had acquired a new dignity. They became the People of God. St. Matthew knew all this, as did every Jew, because this was the great event in their history. They sang of it in their songs; it was the theme of their poetry, the subject of their prayer. They celebrated it with a solemn meal every year; it was the foundation of their hope that what God had done once, he would *God is* do again. God is Saviour. God is Love. And when his *Saviour . . .* people are in subjection he will come to their aid. Could it be that this man Jesus who had now come would throw off the yoke of the Romans?

Slowly St. Matthew learnt that indeed this man had come to save; to found a kingdom and make a new People of God; but it was only gradually that he came to the realisation of these things. St. Matthew was a humble man. He knew his limitations and that the more a man is a sinner the more he needs God; the more he feels inadequate the more he wants help. The Pharisees, poor fools, trusted in themselves. 'We don't need to be saved' was their attitude. Poor fools indeed. They had missed the point.

You and I, dear brethren, can easily miss the point. You think because you don't find prayer easy; because attendance at Mass is not congenial; because your record in the service of God is not a good one, that the things of God are not for you. Can't you see that the more inadequate you are, the more you need God's help? You and I are not likely to make the mistake of the Pharisees. We are not likely to say: 'I don't

need to be saved'; but we are likely to get into a frame
of mind whereby we say: 'I don't want to be saved';
and when a man reaches that he is in a sorry state.
There is a yearning in me for security and happiness,
half-conscious, unconfessed—a yearning, although I
don't know it, for God. It is this which God wishes
to use. My heart will be restless until it rests in him.

21. 2. 64

'*I am the Resurrection and the Life*'[1]

What if life had nothing to offer but death? Nothing
other than this world's goods and transient happiness?
The world gives quick returns but these are cheated by
death. For those whose only preoccupation is to seek
pleasure and fame and success, death is the final and
the greatest tragedy. No, we want to live, to live fully,
to go on living. If only death could be conquered! If
only the sting could be taken out of it! That, precisely,
is what our Lord has done.

It is a twofold death which he has conquered. For
there are two kinds of death. There is death which is
separation of body and soul—physical death. But there
is also a death which is separation between man and
God. This is spiritual death. Spiritual death befalls a
person who deliberately chooses to live as if God did
not exist; who deliberately chooses to disobey God in
a matter of grave importance. Now these two deaths
are intimately connected. It was because our first
parents deliberately chose to disobey their Creator that
they died spiritually; and the punishment for their
rebellion was physical death. The tragedy is, hard
though it is to understand, that we, their descendants,
are involved. You and I were born 'dead', separated
from God, destined to be deprived of that vision which
alone can satisfy our deepest aspirations.

Our Lord overcame both kinds of death. How did
he do this? By himself dying and rising again from the
dead. He died in very truth. He died a physical death,
enduring thereby the punishment for sin which is the
lot of all mankind. But in him there was no separation
from God as in spiritual death. This is a great mystery.

[1] John 11:25.

He allowed himself to undergo the misery of being separated from his heavenly Father: 'My God, my God, why have you forsaken me?' But on the third day he rose from the dead. More than that, human nature in him came out of the tomb renewed and radiant! This spiritual life—sometimes called supernatural life, more often called grace—he wants to give to us all. He wants to give us that life, whereby here and now, we can enjoy friendship with him and ultimately be granted *Friendship* the vision of God which alone, as I have said, can *with him*. satisfy our deepest aspirations.

He wants to give us life; and he wants to renew that gesture whereby he restored life to the son of the widow of Naim, to the daughter of Jairus, to his friend Lazarus. To them, he restored physical life; to us, by a like gesture, he restores spiritual life. The Sacraments are the means by which our Lord touches us and gives this life—gives it when we do not possess it, and gives it more fully where he already finds it. But if we choose to reject it, then, dearest brethren, we live 'dead'. We live a life which is fundamentally meaningless because it is bound by horizons of this present world, destined ultimately to frustration, to misery. To live separated from God is indeed to live 'dead'.

Pray God that we who are baptised and given life by Christ himself may so live in union with him that when we meet physical death we shall die 'alive'.

28. 2. 64

'From death to life'

Salvation means passing from death to life. That is, passing from a state of separation from God to union with him. And this life, as we saw, comes to us precisely because our Lord himself passed from death to life: died and rose again. We saw too, that this life is given to us first in baptism, by which we are enabled to enjoy friendship with God here and now; and later, when we pass through physical death, we shall come to that vision which alone can satisfy our deepest aspirations. By living with this life—indeed living this life—we become God-centred rather than self-centred. Rather than living a life in which only material success and worldly pleasures matter, we now live in reference to God. Ours is the choice to live 'dead', to live separated from God; but if we choose to live for him, then we live that life which Christ gives us—indeed with the very life of Christ himself within us.

But our blessed Lord must be at work on us all the time. His saving power must always be operating in our regard in order to check those forces which make for separation from God. There is not one of us who has not experienced in himself the very real possibility that something could drive him away from God; so at every moment we need to be saved from making fools of ourselves in the eyes of God. After all, our natural life is sustained by a constant willing by God. Were God to cease to will us, we would return to the nothingness from which we came. If that is so of natural life, how much more true will it be of the life with which we have been re-created in Christ. His life-giving touch is held out constantly to us and we can refuse to be touched. If we refuse, for instance, to make use of the Sacraments we are refusing to be touched by our Lord. We are choosing to live 'dead'.

There must be constant contact with Christ. Being a Christian does not merely mean observing a certain code of behaviour; it does not mean merely using our Lord as our model. It does mean both these things indeed; but being a Christian means becoming involved in the life of Christ or, to put it the other way round, allowing Christ to become involved in my life. There must be a meeting of person with person, a mutual involvement of the one with the other. Being in contact with Christ will entail also being in contact with Christ's work, with what he has done. It means being in contact with his work of redemption; the work of salvation he has wrought on your behalf and mine; it means being in contact with his Passion, Death, and Resurrection.

He bridged the gulf . . .

What did our Lord do by his Passion, Death, and Resurrection? He bridged that gulf which exists between God and man, a gulf which can only be bridged by him. He is indeed truly a pontifex: the Builder of the bridge. He is the mediator between God and man precisely because he is both God and Man. But at his death on the Cross he was giving to God his Father all that is human. He offered himself, and as he offered himself he offered each one of us. At the same time he gave to man, or willed to give to man, a share in the divine life. It is the rôle of Christ to give to God the things of man and to man the things of God. Thus the Passion, Death, and Resurrection are the central points of all history, and each individual must be brought into contact with that work of Christ.

In the last three days of Holy Week we think about these truths. We think about the Passion, the Death, and the Resurrection of our Lord. We are not merely enacting an historical pageant, not merely recalling historical events—we make them present so that we have some share in them. The Mass in particular makes the work of Christ present to us. With divine delicacy God puts at our disposal the work of Christ, so that we can become involved. This is the particular significance of Maundy Thursday, because on that day our Lord gave us the Mass. On that day he assembled with his apostles to celebrate the paschal supper. This meal, you remember, had been celebrated by the Jews for some 1,250 years to commemorate that complex of events which we call the Exodus—the deliverance from Egypt. It took place to evoke their gratitude and to remind them of their dependence on God.

It was at that paschal meal that our Lord took bread and changed it into his Body, took wine and changed it into his Blood, so that this meal should commemorate events more decisive, more important than those concerned with what we call the Exodus. What our Lord wanted to be remembered was his Passion, Death, and Resurrection. There was a great difference between the two meals. The first merely commemorated past events. The Mass does more: it makes present the Passion, Death, and Resurrection of our Lord through symbols: the consecrated Bread and the consecrated Wine. You and I could not have devised a way of making the Passion, Death, and Resurrection present for all men for all time; only God could devise what he has, in fact, devised. For, every time the Mass is said, the sacrifice of Calvary is repeated. Every time you receive Holy Communion the life of the risen Christ is given to you. We witness two things: the gift of man to God and the gift of God to man. It is Christ who gives himself to his Father together with ourselves; and it is Christ who is given to us in Holy Communion.

On Good Friday we think about the offering of our Lord on the Cross. On Holy Saturday we think about the resurrected life. So you can see already how the chief theme of these three days is in fact precisely the theme of the Mass.

3. 3. 64

'This is my Beloved Son'[1]

In Holy Week we think about the Passion, Death and Resurrection of our Lord. We are not, I have said, merely recalling historical events. We are not just re-enacting a pageant. with no meaning. We are doing what we do in order that we may ourselves participate in the work of Christ. Our Lord was offering himself to God his Father: offering his love which he expressed through obedience – obedience even unto death. At the same time, he was passing through death to life, that you and I might share in his risen life. We have to be involved in the offering of love which Christ made on the Cross. In the sacrifice of the Mass we are provided with that opportunity. Through the Sacraments, especially the Eucharist, we receive the risen life of Christ: indeed in Holy Communion we receive the very author of that life. Our chief thought on Maundy Thursday will be the institution of the Mass. On Good Friday we shall think of the offering our Lord made of himself to his heavenly Father. On Holy Saturday we shall think of that risen life in which we share. In a sense, every time the Mass is celebrated, Holy Week is contained in its entirety.

This evening we will think about Good Friday. Clearly we shall have to be selective. My mind goes back to the first Palm Sunday. I like to think of St. Peter walking in that triumphal procession, thinking that things were really going well. A sense of pride: people rushing out, laying their garments and palms along the way upon which our Lord was passing. They were crying: 'Hosanna to the Son of David. Blessed is he who comes in the name of the Lord.' And then he

[1] Luke 9:35.

would remember prophecies there had been: 'Behold, your king shall come sitting on an ass.' A sense of pride. It was all going to come right.

Then I like to think of Peter remembering how our Lord had stood upon the mountain and been transfigured before himself, St. James, and St. John. His face had shone like the sun, his garments were white as snow. Then a cloud appeared—the sign, for a Jew, of the presence of God—and a voice said: 'This is my beloved Son.' Our Lord had been there, with Elias and Moses. Then they had come down from the mountain and life had gone on as usual. I like to think too that St. Peter's mind travelled to a vision recorded in the Book of Daniel: 'I beheld in the vision of the night, and lo, one like the son of man came upon the clouds of heaven. And he came even to the ancient of days: and they presented him before him. And he gave him power and glory and a kingdom: and all the tribes, peoples, and tongues shall serve him. His power is an everlasting power that shall not be taken away: and his kingdom shall not be destroyed.' This magnificent figure was surely that of the Son of Man appearing in all his majesty to found a kingdom, a kingdom of all the elect. Might not St. Peter have had all this in mind as our Lord rode into Jerusalem? Now the Roman power would be overthrown. Now the enemies of the Lord among the Jews would be silenced once and for all—no matter that here at this very moment they were plotting against him. This was the moment of triumph.

Then a week passes. All is changed. They are not *A king?..* shouting 'Hosanna' now: they are shouting 'Crucify him! Crucify him!' A king? Why, he is crowned with thorns. Transfigured? Garments white as snow? Covered with spittle, blood, and sweat. A prophet come to teach? Why, at Herod's palace they treated him like a fool. Poor Peter. Doubts cloud his mind. Disillusionment. He cannot run away completely. He hangs around, wondering why it's so difficult to persevere when the Master is now, it seems, in the hands of his enemies.

And Judas? Ah, he was right. Success and pleasures *Poor* of this world? Thirty pieces of silver: he has all these *Judas ...* now. And, our Lord? Well, it was a dream; he had been misled for a short time, but he was right; he knew; he had an idea all the time that he was right. Poor Judas.

And then Pilate appears with our Lord: '*Ecce Rex vester*': 'Behold your King!' Crowned with thorns, covered with spittle, treated as a fool. 'Behold your King!' That point had worried Pilate. He had cross-questioned our Lord about this claim to kingship. Indeed Christ's enemies among the Jews used just this point to get a conviction. Here is a man rivalling Caesar. Here is a man who could overthrow the Romans. Pilate is frightened. 'Behold your King!' And then over the gallows, the cross upon which our Lord will hang, they will put an inscription in three languages: 'Jesus of Nazareth, King of the Jews.' 'No,' said the Jews, 'don't put that; say rather, he *said* he was the King of the Jews.' Pilate: *Quod scripsi, scripsi*. 'What I have written, I have written.' And Pilate, who knew least of all about these things, had got it right. This indeed was the King of the Jews.

Peter seems to have forgotten, as indeed had the Jews who plotted against our Lord's life, that the kingdom would be founded, not through power, not through manifestation of majesty, but precisely this way. It's strange how all of our Lord's contemporaries had forgotten that vision of Isaias: Isaias who saw a man

in whom there was no beauty, no sightliness, that we should be desirous of him; despised and the most abject of men; a man of sorrows and acquainted with grief, and his look was as it were hidden and despised. Whereupon we esteemed him not. Surely he has borne our infirmities and carried our sorrows. And we have thought him as it were a leper, and as one struck by God and afflicted . . . He shall be led as a sheep to the slaughter and shall be dumb as a lamb before his shearer, and he shall not open his mouth.

This was the King who would found his kingdom, through his suffering and through his death. In our Lord himself were united the two prophecies: Daniel's vision of the Son of Man and the vision of Isaias of the Suffering Servant. 'And now he began to make it known to them that the Son of Man must be much ill-used, be rejected by the elders and chief priests and scribes, be put to death and rise again after three days.' And later, during his Passion, our Lord says: 'And you will see the Son of Man sitting at the right hand of God's power, coming on the clouds of heaven.' Yes indeed. How often he had called himself the 'Son of Man'— showing that he was fulfilling the prophecy of that mighty figure whom Daniel has seen in a vision. How often had he preached that the Kingdom of God was near at hand. How often had he compared heaven to the Kingdom. And here, now, at that very moment he was founding the Kingdom through suffering, through death . . . Meaningless, had it not been for the triumph of his Resurrection. As he hung on the Cross a new alliance was made between God and man. The Bridge-Builder was indeed bridging the gulf which separates man from God. He was making retribution for the enormity of the insult which sin is. He was, as Priest, offering himself as Victim in a new sacrifice which would seal in his blood the new Covenant with God. A new people of God was born. Peter wept and was saved. Judas? . . . Poor Judas.

13. 3. 64

VII

Mary

1. '. . . To listen, to receive, to watch . . .'

'His Mother pondered all these things in her heart . . .'[1]

A WOMAN IN THE CROWD called out, 'Blessed is the womb that bore you and the breasts that gave you suck'[2] and so proclaimed the dignity of the body which has borne the Son of God. We should always think with respect and admiration of the body that is called to the noble task of bringing forth life. But in this instance it is the body of our Lady, noble beyond all others, in that, rightly and properly, it was so fashioned that it might be worthy of the purpose for which God had chosen her. 'Blessed rather', our Lord said, 'are those who hear the word of God and keep it,' thereby seeming to commend a yet higher dignity of hers: that she heard the word of God and lived by it – she who listened, then pondered in her heart.

It is a feminine trait to listen, to receive, to watch. Perhaps that is why more women pray than men. Perhaps that is why among contemplatives there are more women than men – it is the 'feminine' which listens and waits. It is a feminine trait, also, to see, to observe. The wine has run out. Mary notices, and being a woman she has a practical mind.

One wonders how intuitive she was. When her Son said words which amount to: 'How does this concern you and me?'[3] – implying it was no affair of hers – did she understand that he was beginning his public ministry in which, for the next two-and-a-half to three years, she would have no part? Did it dawn on her that from now

[1] Luke 2:51.
[2] Luke 11:27.
[3] John 2:4.

160

onwards there would be separation—the trial which every mother must face, unless she is to ruin her child? 'My hour has not yet come': the hour when he will pass from death to life and she will again be united to him.

Such then she is: controlled, free, noble; sensitive in her capacity to listen, quick to notice the needs of others, generous in her practical help, keen in her perceptivity. All that is finest in woman has not been better realised than in her—Mary, who was immaculately conceived. From the moment when her life took its beginning in the womb of her mother, St. Anne, she was destined to be unique among the children of God. We make a grave mistake in our spiritual lives if she has no part. It is at our peril if we fail to understand her rôle in the life of her Son and in our own lives. Immaculately conceived, she is able to love as can no other creature: she has loved the God whom—tradition tells—she served from early childhood, the Son whom she bore, and ourselves who, by this same Son, were commended to her at the most solemn moment of his life.

7. 12. 71

2. 'Fiat'

'I have called you by your name.'[1]

Our Lady must have been surprised by the message she had received from the angel. She was to become a mother, she was told. But was not that impossible, since she had chosen a life of virginity? Besides even if that had not been so, why should she be singled out to be the mother of the long-expected, eagerly-awaited Messiah? Surely there were women more suitable than she in Israel? No wonder she was deeply disturbed.

How often it is like this when God intervenes in a human life—when the unexpected and the impossible happen. And the first reaction to that kind of intervention is often one of fear: it can grip, almost paralyse! What is needed is a reassuring word or gesture, a *Do not be* healing word: 'Do not be afraid, Mary. You have won *afraid . . .*

[1] Isa. 43:1.

God's favour.'¹ That word of divine love—for such it
is—has a special, unique quality. It not only reassures,
it liberates, gives life, inspires. Brother, can you hear
the word being said to you at this moment, as you
await your Profession? 'Do not be afraid, you have won
God's favour.'² At the level where only God can
penetrate, I believe you can.

For six years now you have pondered and prayed: we
have done likewise. You have decided and so have we
that, as far as we can tell, God has called you to follow
Christ in the monastic way. At times his intervention
may have seemed to you unexpected and impossible.
'Do not be afraid.' The decision was not taken lightly
by you or by us. None of us had a vision which made
God's will for you self-evident. Nor did our Lady have
any such vision: she had to put her trust in a messenger,
as you have had to put your trust in the experience and
wisdom of your brethren. God uses intermediaries.

In a moment you will pronounce your *Fiat*, your
'Yes': 'Let it be done to me according to your word.'³
The declaration of your vows is your answer to God's
call to you: it is business-like and canonical in its form,
but the love in the depths of your being will make
those dry legal bones live—not necessarily today: but
day by day this Profession will mean more and more
to you.

Did Mary know how it would work out once she had
said her *Fiat*, her 'Yes'? She did not. Nor do you. God's
love can be demanding and purifying, but also warming
and encouraging. And surely it is the experience of all
the saints that the greater the demands, the greater the
proofs of his love: 'You have won God's favour.'

'Do not be afraid, for I have redeemed you, I have
called you by your name: you are mine.
Should you pass through the sea, I will be with you,
or through rivers, and they will not swallow you up,
Should you walk through fire, you will not be
scorched, and the flames will not burn you.
For I am the Lord, your God, the Holy One of
Israel, your Saviour.'⁴

¹ Luke 1:30.
² ibid.
³ Luke 1:38.
⁴ Isa. 43:1–3.

Let these words of the prophet Isaiah ring in your ears.

'May the power of the Spirit which sanctified Mary, the Mother of your Son, make holy the gift of yourself upon this altar.'
(Prayer over offerings, IV Sunday of Advent.)

21. 12. 75

VIII

Experiencing God

1. Vulnerability of God

EVERY AGE PRODUCES its particular expression of the Christian truth. Our age produces different manifestations. The Focolari movement, for instance, seems to be in part a reaction to the impersonal character of modern urban society, and is the expression of the desire for inter-personal relationships which come from other quarters, in terms of philosophy. Transcendental meditation is, I think, a reaction to over-verbalised forms of prayer, and corresponds to the need for silence and wholeness within. The Charismatic movement is in part a reaction to the Church's rigid and perhaps over-structured and over-loaded system of law: it corresponds to the aspirations people have for freedom and joy of expression in their spiritual lives.

In the seventeenth century the cult of the Sacred Heart was a reaction to Jansenism—that narrowing down of the possibility of salvation which was supposed to characterise the elect. It was a Calvinistic counterpart in the Catholic Church. It is not altogether inappropriate to talk about it to a Benedictine community for, as you know, in the thirteenth century, it is said, St. John the Evangelist appeared to St. Gertrude and told her of the significance of the beating of the heart of Jesus which he heard while resting his head on our Lord's breast—the meaning of which was to be revealed in its fullness when our Lord appeared to St. Margaret Mary at Paray-le-Monial in June 1675, at a time when the world had grown cold in its appreciation of God's love. Many may not feel attracted to the devotion of the Sacred Heart as presented at the end of the nineteenth century and the beginning of this, but the theology behind the devotion is of the first importance. We would do well, as a stimulus to prayer, to take the antiphons for Vespers and Lauds.

There are two points I would like to make. First, the Sacred Heart makes divine love human, interprets divine love in human language; for the Word made flesh speaks not only in verbal communication, but also in terms of divine qualities alive in human experience.

May I draw your attention to a quotation from the Gospel. Our Lord had cured the mother of Simon Peter's wife. The sun was going down and those who had friends afflicted with illness brought them to him, and 'he laid his hands upon each one of them'.[1] Personal, individual attention. We know our Lord's attitude towards a vast number of persons with whom he came into contact, irrespective of their station, their moral probity, whether they were attractive or not. That personal attention reveals in a striking manner what we know is true of God himself. For each one of us it should be a source of comfort and help: God has this individual concern for me, irrespective of my weaknesses, irrespective of my shortcomings.

Secondly, the feast of the Sacred Heart reveals the vulnerability of God. It is difficult for those who are Thomists to use, of God, the word 'vulnerability'. How can an unchanging God be vulnerable? It is only in his Son made man that we can get a glimpse of this. Again, one can produce a list of situations in which our Lord showed his vulnerability: his reaction to the ingratitude of the nine lepers; his weeping over Jerusalem; his grief at the death of Lazarus; his evident affection for Martha and Mary; and his reaction to his betrayal by Judas; 'You betray the Son of Man with a kiss?' Read the Gospels again and again, and you will encounter the vulnerability of our Lord. It seems that God became man to feel what man can feel, to show that he understands. And we can see, since Christ's humanity is part of him and part of the life of the Trinity, how there can be vulnerability in the Trinity itself. *... to show that he understands ...*

It was to St. Gertrude, so it is said, that St. John talked about the Sacred Heart: St. John, we may say, is the theologian of the Sacred Heart. The Office of the Sacred Heart lays stress on the piercing of Christ's

[1] Luke 4:40.

side and the outpouring of water and blood. This was
his moment of glory, his hour: the water is a symbol of
the Holy Spirit; the blood, the Holy Eucharist. Christians down the ages, contemplating the pierced side of
Christ, have witnessed at that moment the birth of the
Church. Movements I referred to earlier—the Focolari
movement with its emphasis on love (the love of God
and love between persons), and the Charismatic movement with its stress on the Holy Spirit and one baptism
in the Spirit, may not suit everyone, but they are movements of which we should be aware if only because
they emphasise that it is in the human heart of Christ
we find the mystery of God's love.

*An inspira-
tion and a
consola-
tion . . .*

That is why we observe the Feast of the Sacred Heart.
We need to come to the first principles of the spiritual
life: the tremendous love God has for each one of us.
The consciousness should not only be an inspiration and
a consolation to ourselves—it should be a model of our
reactions to each other. The concern and compassion
we should have for every member of the Community
is extremely important. It does not matter how divided
a community is, how diverse in its practices and ideo-
logies—none of that need matter, although it can be,
at one level, regrettable. What does matter is that there
should be real charity, real love, real concern, real interest in one another. Everyone in the Community has
to be my concern: there must be a real generosity, a
readiness to put myself out for others, to deny myself
for others. I think, Fathers, we need to pray urgently
that the love which God shows us should be passed
on from one to another in this Community and through
us to all with whom we have contact. A Christian
community should be a loving community. The work
within a community presupposes sacrifice: it is easy to
opt out, to be selective with those with whom we are
in contact. That is not right at the level of Christian
living: it is certainly not right on the monastic level. It
is exhausting to be constantly giving, constantly available. But that is the grace for which we must ask. That
is the way of the Lord, the way of our Father in heaven;
and we, with all our deficiencies, must strive to be
perfect, even as our heavenly Father is perfect.

3. 6. 75

2. Mother Julian of Norwich: three wounds: contrition, compassion, longing for God

The thoughts I would like to put to you, Fathers, form a sort of pastiche or collage of readings which we have heard in the past day or two: a passage from Mother Julian of Norwich, some extracts from the ordination rite, and one or two we have had today. They suggest, I think, some important truths.

Early in her 'Revelations' Mother Julian says: 'Through the grace of God and the teaching of Holy Church I developed a strong desire to receive three wounds: namely, the wound of true contrition, the wound of genuine compassion, and the wound of sincere longing for God.'[1] This passage struck me while I was thinking about the priesthood and the great event which took place on Sunday, and the qualities a priest should have. It occurred to me that Mother Julian's three desires were vital.

None of us approaching the priesthood or looking back on our priestly lives can be devoid of a sense of *Contrition...* contrition when we think of our sinfulness and unworthiness. This should characterise our spirituality and it is very far from being a depressing thought. We should never allow ourselves to be overwhelmed by our unworthiness, our sinfulness: we must always cling to the thought that God is incapable—if I may put it this way—of exercising his wonderful power of forgiveness if there is nothing to forgive, and that our sinfulness is a claim on his power of forgiveness which is part of his loving concern. And so it is a thought which should leave a sense of contentment and peace. If we are not aware of our sinfulness it is either because we have a wrong notion of sin or, worse, a wrong view of ourselves; or, in the case of a priest, we do not value sufficiently the awesomeness of the vocation to which we have been called—we never could. But God does not wish us to be depressed, otherwise he would not have called us; he would not have instituted the priesthood.

I wondered why Mother Julian talked about the wound of sincere longing, the wound of contrition, the wound of genuine compassion. In what sense was she

[1] Rev. 2.

using the word 'wound'? In connection with contrition it is, I suppose, inevitably, self-knowledge – the revelation of one's sinfulness and unworthiness is, in a sense, a wound. But it is not so much the wound of the Cross as the wound of the resurrected Christ. That is the way to see these wounds; that is where we find our hope, our peace, our consolation. A practical point arises from this: it is a pity, I think, that in the life of the Church (and possibly in the life of monks) confession has diminished, or is less important. It is very difficult to find, I believe, a real substitute for going on one's knees before a representative of God to avow one's unworthiness and sinfulness. We do not do so to win peace: it is a practical and sensible way of saying 'sorry' to God. But it brings, and should bring, its own peace.

*Compas-
sion . . .*

The wound of genuine compassion. To be able to listen and to listen sympathetically is compassion – and to be able to suffer with other people: these are qualities we recognise in priests who have a large pastoral influence. The reading we had after Matins (Col. 3) struck me: 'Take care not to let anyone cheat you with his philosophising, with empty phantasies drawn from human tradition, from worldly principles – they were never Christ's teaching' (Knox). I do not think one would quarrel with St. Paul on that. It is important that we should, in exercising our compassion, in exercising our priesthood through counselling, through helping others, be able to give the teaching of Christ, to offer a word which often is paradoxical – as the words of Christ can be. To be able to communicate the word of Christ is to communicate the sympathy of Christ, the strength of Christ.

'The word of God' – this thought struck me too. It was a remark of Lord Hailsham's: I seem to remember it as 'the soul of oratory is sincerity'. Actually it was, I think, 'the soul of rhetoric is sincerity'; but it is better to say 'the soul of oratory is sincerity'. In the whole question of communicating the word of God it is sincerity that matters: not the clever thought, the neat turn of phrase. What matters is genuine sincerity, which can come through the most banal thought and the clumsiest sentence. How often it is true that it is the *man* to whom one is listening, not the words he is saying. And surely sincerity has to be the quality of a person who is in contact with Christ our Lord.

The wound of sincere longing for God. No need to develop that theme. You have heard it so often—that nostalgia for prayer, that relentless search for God which is fundamental in our monastic life. You remember the story of our Lord in the boat with the disciples. He falls asleep, and the disciples call: 'Lord, save us, we are sinking.' And then our Lord's rebuke. It pulls us up short: 'Why are you faint-hearted, men of little faith?'[1] And that, I suppose, is the danger for every Christian—and the danger therefore for every priest—to be timorous because one has too little faith. Faith gives a priest his power to act and his inspiration. And we know from experience that faith is not something we bring forth ourselves: it is something we receive, which is given to us. It is something for which we have to dispose ourselves and pray. There can, I think, be few better aspirations for a priest than Mother Julian's prayer: contrition, which gives us the proper attitude of humility to God; genuine compassion, which gets our relationship with others right in our ministry and pastoral work; and our longing for God, which is its crown as also its inspiration.

Longing for God . . .

2. 7. 74

3. Inner Hurts

We have had discussions latterly on the new rite of Penance, and on sin. We have a long way to go, not only to understand these things but to be able to communicate them to those for whom we are responsible. Moreover, our discussions have led me to think a great deal about the ministry of healing. Although I am no expert in the matter and have an innate tendency to approach this with circumspection, I think none the less there is something here for us to consider; furthermore, it brings in considerations which will be helpful to our lives with Christ.

We are conditioned, I suspect, to think that the miracles of our Lord as recorded in the Gospels are 'proofs' of his divinity, or incidents to be demythologised (on the Bultmann assumption that miracles cannot happen), or 'pieties' introduced by early Christians

[1] Matt. 8:26.

for the benefit of Jewish and Greek communities whom
they were addressing. Yet in the back of our minds
there lurks the thought that Christ does indeed have
power and that this power can and will work through
the Sacraments and perhaps in answer to prayer. But
we are not totally convinced.

Re-read the first chapter of St. Mark's Gospel:
'Jesus came into Galilee preaching the Gospel of God's
Kingdom. The appointed time has come and the Kingdom of God is near at hand: repent and believe the
Gospel.' There follows the calling of some of his disciples
and the teaching in the synagogue. And after that? We
are told about a series of healings: a man possessed
with an unclean spirit; Simon Peter's wife's mother;
then a whole crowd of persons; and at verse forty the
story of the leper: 'If it be your will, you have power to
make me clean.'

The Kingdom is proclaimed, the programme is clear:
repent, and accept the good news. But there is also
healing. What does Jesus want to heal and why? Let
us take the first question. There are different kinds of
ills and suffering, and their causes are no less varied.
Every kind of suffering can be used profitably: accepted
as a Cross, it is redemptive. There are, however, 'ills'
which do not profit—can, indeed, be harmful. I refer
to those within, which gnaw at us, leaving us limp and
less effectual for God's work—thwarted ambition,
resentment, frustration, wounds inflicted by other
people, the pain that comes from feeling unappreciated,
disliked, rejected; criticism, too, which is unfair. These
can leave wounds that fester. They need to be healed.
Why? Because they enslave and sadden, whereas
Christ's mission was to bring freedom and happiness.
If we are paralysed by 'inner hurts' we can turn inwards
upon ourselves, and then we are unable to help others,
to carry burdens; or we are not free to be totally at the
disposal of Christ. Yes, these inner wounds must be
healed.

Why do we go on labouring under unprofitable
stresses in spite of the Sacraments and prayers in which
we have asked for God's help? Christ cannot heal
where there is no faith or where someone lacks the
conviction that he has the power to heal and wants to
do so. Mechanical confessions or routine reception of

Holy Communion can have little impact, little effect. 'It is my will, be made clean.' We must believe in Christ's power to heal and in his will to do so. But conviction is a gift and must be asked for. 'Lord, I believe. Help my unbelief.'[1] 'Which is easier, to forgive, or to say "Take up your bed and walk"?'[2] Christ, by healing him, proved to the paralytic that he had been forgiven. Forgiveness and healing go together.

The Gospel is not only a programme for action, it is also a proclamation of the power at our disposal. Moreover, forgiving and healing should characterise our treatment of each other. Christ's manner of action has to be the model for ours. As pastors, we need to learn how to use his healing power, or how to be *His healing* instruments enabling him to exercise that power on one *power . . .* another. Just as I tend to believe that most people are sick rather than sinful, so too I think that the most corrosive factor in any community or family are the wounds which we unwittingly inflict on each other. Those need forgiveness and healing: Christ's forgiveness and healing, and ours too. In both cases forgiving and healing are an expression of God's love at work in us and among us.

How may one summarise all this? Christ came not only to proclaim a message but to use a healing power. He wishes to heal because we have wounds which paralyse genuine love: wounds that make us deaf to his word, blind to what he wants us to see. His healing brings happiness and freedom so that we can carry our burdens and serve more faithfully.

In spiritual reading we can choose episodes telling how our Lord heals, and we can mull over them. They provide endless food for thought. Pray privately psalms 29 and 30[3] (30 comes better before 29). And if your own situation is serene and untroubled, then think of your family, the Community, or your friends, whose mouthpiece you can be. Those thoughts can help in administering the Sacraments, especially the Sacrament of Penance and of the sick. We begin to see new meaning in them. Among ourselves as a monastic community

[1] Mark 9:24.
[2] John 5:8.
[3] Psalms 29 and 30 (R.C. editions).=Psalms 30 and 31 (Authorised Version).

striving to live out the Gospel, compassion and concern should be translated into acts. At the root of most people's problems is 'insecurity' and with this goes fear. Insecurity needs to be healed with compassion and concern, so that love may cast it out. Secure in Christ, a Christian can be effective.

11. 11. 75

4. Inner Healing

Christ's healing power should be exercised on those problems which are corrosive of internal peace and happiness—wounds that need to be healed. Reflect on this within the context of living together: a good and happy community depends on the recognition of a basic need in each individual—namely, that a person should know he is loved not for anything he can do, but simply because he is as he is. That realisation of being loved, respected, wanted, appreciated, is the foundation on which is built an authentic spiritual life. Such a life begins with an understanding of what I mean by God. In community living the same principle operates: I know myself to be respected, wanted, and appreciated by others and I strive to respect, want, and appreciate them. To live up to this ideal presupposes a transformation within ourselves, a putting aside of the old self—the self which can preoccupy our entire mind, occupy the centre of every stage. It is better to say 'Yes' to others than 'No' to oneself: none the less the former often demands the latter.

Thus, a constant inner healing of wounds inflicted, which includes a real forgiveness of each other and endless understanding leads to a real respect for, a wanting and an appreciation of all others. This is the secret of living in community for it is putting on the mind of Christ and living as he told us that we should: 'forgive us our trespasses as we forgive others.'

There can be no love among brethren unless there is companionship, a being together, a doing together. The nature of our work and life-style tends to make us individualistic: individual activities, sometimes in competition with one another, can have this effect. Not that individual activities are to be condemned: the need to express ourselves in our work, the desire to have something to show, a style of life that recognises differences of talents, temperaments, and tastes—this is desirable. But there must be occasions which allow brotherly love to be fostered. Companionship, as well as being the cause of love, is its handmaid.

Praying together is important. On a previous occasion I welcomed—and do so again now—groups that pray together, come together because of an affinity either of persons or outlook. That is good. But what of the prayer where we are thrown together—how does brotherly love work here? Why can it be a strain for some, a delight to others? Why do some seek opportunities to be absent, are relieved when they need not be present? These are causes for sadness, especially as solutions which please some, sadden others.

Community prayer must necessarily be inadequate: group prayer tends to be a better means of expressing self, while Choir prayer often appears as a suppression of self. Yet I do not accept the apparent antithesis. Suffice it to say that a total involvement in what takes place in Choir is the way to discover its value. Distaste and irritation make it burdensome. The solution? A sense of companionship in our being together, an over-riding desire to please God informing our desire not to displease each other, a forgiving and tolerant attitude; sensibility to the difficulties of others—these are basic. There are, of course, inequalities in our capacities. But apart from the adjustments each has to make, it is the 'attitude' that matters: this is the work of God. If it cannot always be given priority amid the conflicting duties of term time, it can during holidays. In Choir, then, as in every aspect of monastic life, the qualities of mutual respect, mutual wanting and appreciation, should prevail.

25. 11. 75

5. Wholeheartedness[1]

We have had to weigh your strengths and your

[1] This chapter was given on the occasion of a Simple Profession ceremony—the last which Abbot Basil gave to his community before the announcement of his appointment to Westminster.

weaknesses in so far as these are relevant to a monastic
vocation. And I would like to say a word about the
weaknesses we all share. When we join a monastic
community we are imperfect beings and remain so
throughout our lives. Such a community has to show a
large degree of tolerance and understanding. We are a
gathering where people come to seek God and we know
that we are far less than perfect. When we take on a
man, we are prepared to show—indeed must show as
Christians—an understanding and tolerance, and expect
to find the same in him. That, I think, is one aspect—
one only—of our vow of stability. We are a family
and you are going to join it through your Profession;
but it is an imperfect family and we can only live
happily and contentedly if there is tolerance and understanding. Monks, I think, are sometimes forgetful of
their duty to be friendly, to be cheerful, to make sure
others are happy and contented. Each one of us bears
responsibility for the happiness of every member of the
Community. That is, after all, only to reflect the
characteristics of God: there is nothing more consoling,
more peaceful, than the divine understanding, the divine
tolerance, the divine forgiveness. And to go further, it
is God's will that we be contented, happy, cheerful:
that is what God wants. There will, it is true, be burdens,
difficulties: it would be surprising if in the cloister this
were not so.

In a phrase I used before, we are 'wounded creatures',
all of us. But, having said that, we have no right to be
complacent. We have a duty to overcome our faults,
make ourselves more lovable in the sight of God and
of men: that is one aspect of our vow of conversion of
manners. We have to change, and the effort can cost
us something; we must have the necessary courage and
sense of purpose. We should want to have our faults
pointed out to us. I would urge you, too, to ponder
as you make your Profession, on the whole-heartedness
of the gift of yourself to God in this Community; on
the whole-heartedness of your following of Christ.
This presupposes a generosity we would show in family
life—if that were our vocation—and must at all costs
be shown within the monastery too. Monks must be
generous, and the test of the generous monk is his
willingness to be obedient. True, this is only one aspect

of monastic obedience, but it is a test of generosity, whole-heartedness, the abandoning of self-seeking, the desire to seek and do the will of God. Most of our problems come from a lack of humility—the hardest quality to acquire, the most lovely to possess. Do not, I beg you, take yourself too seriously. Laugh at yourself. And let others laugh at you and with you. This is part of family life!

23. 1. 76

6. Enthusiasm

I said to you a while ago that my life was passing through a difficult phase. I asked myself whether I was being too worldly, living in too worldly a way, becoming too easy-going and whether, as a consequence, the 'spine' had gone out of my prayer. I said, you will perhaps remember, that it is difficult to define what one means by 'worldly'; that, in fact, it is a monastic instinct which tells us, it seems, what is fitting and what is not fitting for a monk. We reminded ourselves that people look for, and expect to see in us, something different which can speak to them of God. We reminded ourselves of the principle in our relationships with others—that we do not seek to identify ourselves with others but seek, rather, to become the kind of person with whom others want to identify. And we talked about being easy-going, and how, if in a community everyone is easy-going, then the community becomes flabby. This is exemplified by our being unpunctual for Office. The first Office of the day is the one which, apart from the difficulty of sleep or sleepiness, provides us with the least excuse for being late. It is wrong that so many of us should arrive late. St. Benedict's reference to the first psalm being said slowly so that people can come in late, is a concession to weakness! We should all be in choir before the knock-up. It is also exemplified in our attitude to silence. I then, you may remember, went on to talk about example and the encouragement we can give to one another, and the importance of enthusiasm. It is about this last that I want to speak.

The opposite of enthusiasm is apathy, staleness, aridity, boredom. But each of these can have a natural explanation: end of term boredom is reason enough. Aridity can be a stage in the purification of faith, or, as we would perhaps put it today, part of the maturing of faith. Nevertheless there should be in our monastic life a joy and an enthusiasm. Where is it to come from? Community discussions, commissions, directives from Superiors, an agreed way of thinking? I would like to look at this in the light of two truths with which our minds are preoccupied at this time of year: the Holy Spirit and the Eucharist.

The ground of our being . . .

First, the Holy Spirit. 'No one has seen the Father.' The Son has ascended into heaven and is no longer present to us through our senses; but the Spirit has been sent and he has been at work in our lives all this time, even though we have not always recognised or realised his presence. Or possibly we recognise his presence insufficiently and for that reason limit the work he can do in us and through us—this same Spirit who teaches, inspires, strengthens, liberates, and alone enables us to say, meaningfully, 'Abba, Father'. We come, I believe, into the presence of the Spirit—which is, after all, the presence of God—mainly through the recognition of our poverty: that poverty which comprises our weakness, our inability to respond to God with warmth and enthusiasm, allowing ourselves to depend too much on our own efforts. There are times when we come to a realisation of the presence of that Spirit in the very depths of our being. I would like to put it this way: at the point where consciousness of self reaches nothingness or touches on the darkness beyond—that is where God is encountered. It is an awareness, as has been well said, of 'the ground of our being'. But in reflecting on the self which I am, there comes a point where one touches on a nothingness beyond. That is the radical poverty where we meet and receive the richness that is God. That poverty, experienced in our nothingness before God, enables us to be receptive to God's action upon us, which is the action of the Spirit.

Pope Leo XIII—he is quoted in the Encyclical *Mystici corporis*[1]—said: 'Christ is the head of the Church and the Holy Spirit is her soul.' I find this a great help, and am delighted to see that the Second Vatican Council

[1] *Mys. cor.* 55.

has said the same: 'The Spirit is one and the same in the head and in the organs. It is he who gives life, unity, and motion to the whole body.' And *Lumen gentium* continues: 'As a result the Fathers have found it possible to compare his work to the function which is fulfilled in the human frame by the principle of life or the soul.'[1]

In another context and on another occasion we reminded ourselves that the head of a monastic community is Christ; consequently it must be the Spirit which animates the community, makes it dynamic and vital. In him above all we must find the principle of 'oneness' within the Community—whatever indeed we lack in ourselves: especially the capacity to respond with enthusiasm and warmth to the message of Christ which is the Gospel. Too little, perhaps, do we pray to the Spirit, too little do we recognise the part he should have in our inner lives and the rôle which is his in our Community by right. To outsiders, apathy, staleness, aridity, boredom, Fathers, sometimes appear to be our response to Conventual Mass. True, it is not the best time of the day at which to be dynamic and vital, and maybe we should have another look at how we do things. But we have to discover the soul of the Mass that gives it life and so brings us to life with it. It is the Spirit which will do this: Christ's Spirit, the Holy Spirit.

Often when we discuss the Eucharist, the Conventual Mass, we talk a great deal about things vital to it as well as other things upon which we should reflect and perhaps take decisions. But all is vain unless, as we stand round the altar, we allow ourselves to be moved by the Spirit. If it is through him only that we can pray: 'Abba, Father', then, *a fortiori*, it seems to me, it is only through him we are able to enter into this most sublime of mysteries.

This does not provide a programme for revitalising our Conventual Mass, but perhaps it gives an opportunity to reflect upon the rôle of each one of us and to pray collectively for the Spirit's guidance. If some of us feel—and I admit I feel with them at times—that there is a poverty in our great act of the day, Conventual Mass; and if this poverty is difficult to resolve because there is such a diversity of views, we can at least agree

[1] L.G.7.

that we are poor, and maybe the answer will be found in our openness to the Spirit and our realisation of our dependence on him. I do not necessarily subscribe to all aspects of Charismatic renewal, but I certainly embrace the theology upon which it is based, and our Community will fall behind—indeed will not meet the demands of true renewal—unless we respond to what seems to be the mood of the day—which is, in our poverty, to invoke the Holy Spirit.

19. 6. 73

7. Awareness of the Love of God

We have a right to be happy: in the first place as Christians, because Christianity must satisfy our deepest human aspirations. And humans seek happiness; practically all their activity can be reduced to that. We know from experience, however, that we are often cheated in our happiness. Human activities, objects, persons, cannot give us the complete unending happiness for which our nature craves. We have to be content with a succession of things or incidents which make us happy, in so far as is possible in this world. If only we could grasp that moment, stop the passage of time, then life would be empty of all that can make it difficult. And that indeed is what eternal happiness will be— unending, and satisfying all our aspirations. It is part of a truly Christian attitude to look forward to enjoying this happiness. The inadequacy of our happiness at the present moment points—unless human aspirations are to remain eternally frustrated—to a happiness that lies beyond this world. It is in God alone we shall find this happiness.

But it would be wrong to conclude that happiness is not something which should be ours now. It would be un-Christian to be suspicious or frightened of things which give us pleasure. We have to learn to see in these the gift of God. Erroneous views have been put forward which have led people to be unreasonably suspicious of the good things of life. And all of us, to a greater or lesser degree, have perhaps unconsciously inherited from our forefathers a jaundiced view of life. And this is not Christian.

Indeed, we ought to consider applicable to ourselves St. Benedict's words in the Prologue: 'As we progress in our monastic life and faith, our hearts shall be enlarged and we shall run with unspeakable sweetness of love in the way of God's commandments.' I used to think this was something to look forward to in the eventide of life. Now I do not think that at all. That 'our hearts shall be enlarged and we shall run . . .' is something which should begin very soon. It is a striking sentence coming in a chapter otherwise uncompromising. It would be wrong to say it is out of character, but it is surprising; it should make us pause and ask ourselves whether this is what is in fact happening . . . because it should. As monks, apart from our being Christians, we have a right to expect happiness here and now.

I would like to talk about this as something at two levels. There is a permanent happiness, deep down, of which we are not always conscious as we go about our daily tasks. This basic contentment comes from a growing awareness of God: an awareness that the things which happen to us are indeed insignificant when measured by the greatness of our task in seeking God. Our search for God (another way of saying 'learning to love', which itself is the byproduct of our understanding of what God's love for us means) gives us a deep contentment of which, I admit, we may not often be aware; it bestows a serenity and security which must grow all the time in our monastic lives.

Then at the other level there are the things, incidents, people which, or who, make up our daily lives. And a great many—indeed all of them—contribute to this sense of contentment, well-being: the ordinary pleasures of life, such as listening to music, a glass of wine, and so on. 'Pleasures,' as C. S. Lewis magnificently puts it, 'are the shafts of the glory of God as it strikes our sensibility.' And then, the worthwhileness of things we do: our work in the school; our work in neighbouring parishes and further afield—all this is satisfying, and rightly so.

But above all, perhaps, is community life. The art of community life is surely to give happiness to others, so that all may share in this happiness. It is the essence of community life to want the happiness of others, to *The happiness of others . . .*

bring about their happiness, participate in their happiness; to avoid anything that might wound another, spoil a relationship, cloud mutual joy. Let us thank God constantly for the joy we find in being a member of this Community.

Read the words in St. Paul's Epistle to the Philippians: 'Rejoice in the Lord always. Again I say rejoice! Let all men know your forbearance! The Lord is at hand. Have no anxiety about anything, but in everything, by prayer and supplication with thanksgiving, let your requests be known to God. And the peace of God which passes all understanding, keep your hearts and minds in Christ Jesus.'[1]

20. 10. 65

8. Happiness

In what does happiness consist? It consists in wanting things and having those wants satisfied. And what is this but to say that happiness consists in loving and being loved! Complete happiness—that for which we were made and the only one that can satisfy—consists, therefore, in loving God and being loved by God. The main problem of Christians and others, it often seems to me, is not so much that they do not love God or do not want to love God or, in trying to love God are conscious of not being successful. The problem consists much more in the fact that we do not allow God to love us. Somehow or other we do not face up to the demands made upon us as a result of realising the extent and intensity of God's love for us. Again, many of us have had a faulty upbringing in the things of God —the emphasis, perhaps, put too much on the punitive, disciplinarian aspects of God, and not on his love. The motive power of our spiritual life, early on, was fear rather than love. Moreover, we fail to allow ourselves to be loved; as a result of ignorance we have not thought sufficiently about God's love. Yet the key to the spiritual life, the authentic beginning, is the realisation of God's love for us. Love calls love. *Abyssus abyssum invocat.*[2]

It is a matter of common experience that we dislike

[1] Phil. 4:4–7.
[2] Psalm 41:8 (R.C. editions).=Psalm 42:8 (Authorised Version).

LIFE IN THE SPIRIT 181

people who dislike us. And the converse is true: we like those who like us. Have you ever found yourself instinctively disliking someone until the day you discovered that he or she rather liked you? Then your attitude begins to change. There are people, too, whom you hold perhaps in contempt, and then you discover that they admire you, and you begin to find things in them which you admire. So when God's love becomes a reality in our minds, then it begins to be a fact in our lives. Then comes our response. It is explicit in St. John's Gospel: 'In this is love, not that we loved God, but that he loved us and sent his Son to be the expiation for our sins.'[1]

Let us think about the nature of God's love. These are simple, elementary truths; but for all their simplicity they call for constant thought. Remember that love is a primary reality: before it is a human fact Love exists in God. Remember that we love people because they are there, but with God it is the other way round: because he loves them they are there. This is an important truth, because it means there is something lovable in all that has been created. It means there is something lovable in every person; if it were not so, that person would not have been created. It is our task to look for whatever is lovable in others.

Again, remember that divine love is the prototype of human love; and so we should have the same attitude towards others as God has towards each one of us. We have to love others because God loves them and finds them lovable. It is well to keep in mind: 'I would not be here unless God loved me.' And to recognise his love is the starting-point of my response. We cannot whip ourselves up to love God as a kind of moral exercise. We have to allow ourselves to be gripped by the thought of his love for us; then, inevitably, we want to respond. I hope this is not too 'unclassical' a reflection on love. I have never been impressed by the various distinctions about love made by the classical philosophers. I wonder whether there can be an *amor amicitiae* without an *amor concupiscentiae* as far as human beings are concerned? I stand subject to correction.

Loving is essentially an outpouring, a giving, a communication. Nowhere is this more fully realised than

[1] 1 John 4:10.

in God. Love is the beginning, therefore, of the whole spiritual life, the beginning of the whole economy of grace.

Let us consider divine love as we see it in our Lord. 'The Word became flesh' translates divine realities into human terms. In the reactions of our Lord and in his activities we see, human-wise, the divine reaction and attitude; we could not have understood these truths except in terms intelligible to man, and so in the Son of God made flesh. Study the attitude of our Lord towards people. See the strength of divine love.

The strength of divine love . . .

When you feel depressed, when life seems not worth living, when everything gets you down, read in the fifteenth chapter of St. Luke the stories of the Prodigal Son and the Lost Sheep. Observe the divine reaction—the stimulant to provide us with the right response.

And so our happiness must consist in loving God and being loved by him. If we fail to respond, it is because we are sometimes afraid of the demands he may make. But it is the law of our being that we should want to be happy, and again, the very law of our being that we should want to love God. God's love is there for us. When our Lord took up the words of God the Father that the first commandment was to 'love the Lord your God with your whole heart, and the second like unto this, to love your neighbour as yourself', he was telling us what in fact is this very law of our being—the only thing that could make sense of life, and so the only thing that can ultimately bring us happiness.

27. 10. 65

9. Inner Peace

All of us feel—some more strongly than others—that it would be a good thing if we could find solutions to many outstanding problems in our Community. Take, for instance, our work for the Church: the contributions we make, be it to the school, to the parishes, as university chaplains—even the possibility of extending the work. This presupposes that we have a true understanding of what the Church is; that we are sensitive to the needs of the modern world; that we have an understanding of the people whom we serve, whether the boys in the school or the communities in the parishes, and that we have a positive idea of what is or should be our contribution as monks, English monks, monks of this Community. Then there are local problems at the level of monastic observance, the liturgy, and various practices in which we engage.

There can be in the present time very differing opinions. Everything can rapidly become an issue and emotions be roused—even clashes can occur. This obtains in the Church as a whole: it would be surprising, therefore, if we were untouched. I think—in fact I am certain—that by and large we don't do too badly: the Community is strong enough to be able to face differences of opinion with a certain equanimity, good sense, and good humour. I wish, though, we could, at all levels, have more consultation. There are things we do as to which we have not yet discovered the correct machinery or methods—I for one find this extremely frustrating. To a large extent the problem—taking the whole conventus—is the enormous spread, geographically, of the Community, with the inevitable consequence of there being so many things which should be discussed in the presence of the entire conventus. It is hard, for example, to discuss parish work if the Fathers involved are not present. Equally it is difficult for those who perhaps have ideas about the school to discuss these without the rest of us being there. It is important to remember that any one part of the conventus is of interest to the whole Community.

Again, the problem of dialogue. Lack of time and energy militate against consultation. It is indeed difficult to put our minds to things when the nature of our work is mentally preoccupying and time-consuming. Then again, the complexity of the issues makes it difficult to talk of these at sufficient length, disentangle the many interrelated problems. Nevertheless we must find ways of consultation, because this is all part of the exercise of collegiality, co-responsibility, participation and involvement which is very much within the Benedictine tradition, very much within the spirit of the Rule.

We are inclined, I think, to underestimate how considerable has been the revolution under which we have lived during the last five or six years: a revolution at once cultural, social, political, and liturgical—and still going on. We need to remind ourselves that a number of us have a good deal that is new to absorb into our thinking, reacting, living. The process of adaptation is going to be slow: we need time to see the implications of what has been happening—this, before we come to decision and action. I see more clearly now—though I instinctively felt it earlier—that it would be a mistake to rush into decisions before we have had time, all of us in our own way, to see the implications. So many questions are being asked, so many assumptions called in question, so many new approaches discovered.

What really matters at such a time is that each of us should find an inner peace and an inner freedom. In the old days we would have called it detachment, but an inner peace and freedom is a more positive way of expressing what I mean. A peace and freedom based on a life of prayer: a life in which reflective reading plays an important rôle: a life in which silence is treasured— in which a monk is able and happy to be at times alone. These are traditional monastic attributes: prayer, reflective reading, a love of silence—an external silence which will help to bring into being an internal silence, a capacity to be alone, to love to be alone with God.

At peace with oneself . . . They are the ingredients too of a good member of a community, because they form a solid basis from which we act in such a way as to relate to other people. For if I do not relate to others on that kind of basis my relating will not be as rewarding as I might suppose. A man on the other hand who is free within and at peace with himself, is not easily ruffled by events, circumstances and people. This peace will not just happen: it is the fruit of a maturity—a monastic maturity and therefore founded on prayer, reflective reading, silence, a capacity to be alone. And I believe firmly that these are qualities which a man needs if he is to be a good member of a community and to relate, in the Christian sense, to others.

This is an ideal towards which we should work, and it can dispose us to be less vulnerable to outside pressures. In making my point I will do so autobiographically. I used to find, and still do so, that if I get worked up, excited about some issue, however trivial, in the school or the monastery, because I am at odds with myself and upset in myself, I seize on this and raise it as a banner. It is easy to do this; it is easy to project my own agonies into other people's situations or find an issue in which I get excited. Really, I mind less about the issue: what is wrong is the fact that I am upset in myself. Now, I have found that when I try to get back to a positive approach, in which reflective reading matters, in which I want to like silence, in which I try to be alone at times with God, then the calm returns, and with the calm comes perspective, and indeed in dealing with issues in which one has to be involved one's persuasiveness increases. That is my experience and I have a suspicion that it might be yours too.

It is important in this period of *aggiornamento*, in this period of divisions and opinions, when there is so much to be tried and achieved, that each should be a man of prayer: a man for whom reflective reading is important, who knows the value of silence, who knows the value of true solitude—and solitude is very different from loneliness. We have to keep working on these things, treasuring them. And then, as I say, we are protected from all kinds of things that upset and disturb us. Only then, I think, are we in a position to be militant—if I may use that word; then we are safe to fight for causes, which indeed we must. And heaven defend us from a community which regards the *status quo* as perfect and does not want to see any change! In the Church today it is not a question of whether we want to change or not; we have been told by the Church that we have to change: we have no option. What we have to change into, what direction we have to take, that is not easy to see, but as the years go by it will become increasingly more clear. It is clearer this year than last; next year it will be even clearer, and so forth.

Finally, remember that it is the present moment *I accept the* which alone is real. It is the present moment alone *present . . .* in which I meet the realities: this present reality which is now mine. It is the present moment in which I meet the Lord, whether in my work or with the person in whose company I am, or in the prayer which I am offering to God—it is in this moment I meet the Lord. And every present moment is a gift from the Lord or an invitation from the Lord for me to respond in love and obedience. And so we go back to the thoughts from St. Paul: that nothing can ever separate us from God —and nothing, as it were, strikes us 'off balance'.

Whether the present moment brings joy or sorrow; whether it brings frustration or sheer delight, I accept the present moment as the moment, as the condition, in which God wills I should meet him. This living in the present is seeking, always, an awareness of God's presence. The building up over the years of this approach not only brings its own enrichment, but in a community it disposes a general calm, a pervading good sense.

One of the tragedies in the modern world is the way in which the clergy in so many regions have lost touch with young people, with youth. Here, where so many of the young live with us, we have from God a privileged position: an opportunity for doing something in the Lord's service. We have tremendous contacts. And on our door-step! The words I use are not a routine flourish; they are said in all sincerity. May God bless us and guide us, and our work be a source of unity and enthusiasm in the Community.

17. 1. 70

10. *Per Jesum Christum Dominum Nostrum*

I want to talk about something—I am almost apologetic about its simplicity—which I presume all of us more or less take for granted. But from time to time a question has to be asked: 'What part does the person of Jesus Christ play in my spiritual life?' It is possible to have a spiritual life based exclusively on ideas or principles and insufficiently on intimacy with the person of Christ. I am not considering the social implications of the Christ event. I am talking about a personal relationship with him. It is the more important in that our monastic life is just one way of following Christ. The implications of the Incarnation and Redemption, his Death and Resurrection, are immense and we should not cease in our meditating on their mysteries to draw important conclusions, to consider the many ways of interpreting those major truths by which we should live. We shall never cease our study of Christ as our model: our reading in the New Testament will show us attitudes and reactions which we should adopt in our lives. Indeed, in studying what he did and what he said, we shall never exhaust the possibilities of discovering more and more. But that is by no means the fundamental aspect of my relationship with him. It has to be one of intimacy and depth. We need also to discover that he is our way to the Father, that he is the Father's way to us. There has to be a growing conviction that salvation comes from him and through him: that he is the very life of our souls.

How does this intimacy develop? There are as many ways as there are people; each person discovers what is right for him or for her. But there are things of particular importance. The initiative, for example, is from our Lord: he wants to know us, and by 'know' I mean he wants to possess the secret of what we are. It is true that his gaze penetrates into us and nothing is hidden from him, but I understand this more as our willingness to abandon ourselves to him, to give ourselves entirely to him. Any inner experience we should share with him. And when you think of it, there is no experience which is entirely personal and exclusively ours, because it will always be shared and known by him. But he must find in us two things. He must find in us a need for him; and this need is learned through the experience of living and as a product of a sustained life of private prayer. He should also find in us that attitude of humility which *Crooks and* we can glean, I think, from making our own certain *crocks . . .* passages of the Gospels concerning two categories of persons: 'crooks' and 'crocks'. The crooks: Matthew, Mary Magdalen, Zacchaeus, the Good Thief, and others. The crocks: the blind man, the deaf, the paralytic, the mute. If you recall the passages about these people you will remember that the impact our Lord has on them seems to prompt two reactions. The first is to follow him; the second, to give glory to God for what has been accomplished. Following Christ, praising God – this, after all, lies at the heart of our monastic vocation. That it should be so is not surprising, for our praise and worship of God is always *per Christum Dominum nostrum.*

8. 10. 74

11. Friendship with God

In thinking and talking about God it is right to use the language of love, since God is Love. And though God is totally other and our minds are unable to grasp his likeness precisely, yet in so far as we are made in his image, there are similarities, there are hints. Besides, Jesus Christ, who is himself the image of the Father, the ikon of God, translates for us in human terms the divine realities.

Two characteristics of friendship concern us here. First, when friendship matures there is less need for frequent contact. What matters is that each should be totally confident of the availability of the other — that he or she is at call when the need arises. Nothing can shake that relationship: it is totally secure. Secondly, there is no fear that our weaknesses will be brought into the open. From acquaintances, we conceal our real selves. To our friends we reveal our weaknesses. True, an excess of self-revelation can destroy the mystery of friendship — but that is another point.

The fact that we are made to the image and likeness of God obtains in the friendship that exists between man and his Creator. It is within our experience to feel the remoteness of God — to feel, at times, abandoned by God. Christ on the Cross knew what it was to feel abandoned by God, but I cannot believe that his confidence in the availability of his Father ever departed from him.

We are often reduced to living on the memory of moments when God's presence was a reality. Yet his presence, as friendship between God and ourselves matures, is one which is increasingly in the background of our lives. There is not necessarily a perpetual contact, because often circumstances make it difficult to have contact, in the sense of a perpetual awareness. But what has to grow is at least an awareness of God in the background. For prayer strengthens and enlivens an awareness which will grow weak in proportion as we do not pray. An awareness of God's presence is the fruit not the cause of prayer. But even when we are leading a serious life of prayer, there will often be an experience of a contact with God which is not continuous.

In God himself there is no weakness — certainly no moral weakness. But let us ponder on this thought: that Christ is the ikon of the Father, the image of the Father, the revelation of the Father, the translation into human terms of divine realities. What a mystery that is when thought of in relation to the Passion and Death of our Lord! It is easier to understand his Passion and Death if we see him as one of us. He is one of us, but he is also one of 'them', by which I mean the Trinity. Does he, when we contemplate his sufferings, in some way reveal to us a divine vulnerability? That phrase needs close scrutiny. If we pursue this line of thinking, perhaps we shall come to some small understanding of the effect on God of the refusal on our part to return love for Love.

A tidy theological mind would baulk at the idea of disappointment or sorrow in an immutable God, but there is a mystery touching on the effect upon God of a failure on man's part to return love for Love. This is revealed to us in the only way we can understand — that is, in human terms: in human experience, which in this case is the experience of Christ. And this principle as a mark of friendship has another consequence in our relationship with God. Our avowal, our admission of guilt, of weakness, to God the Father is an act of love. This must be the basis, the root of the Sacrament of Penance.

These, then, are thoughts based on the experience of human friendship to help us to understand something of the mystery which is God. We have the revelation of God in Christ; we have the revelation of God in the word of God, the Scriptures; but in human experience, because we are made in the image and likeness of God, we can find something of him in ourselves.

26. 3. 71

IX

Sermon delivered by Father Abbot at the Sunday Mass of 22nd February 1976, six days after the announcement of his elevation to the See of Westminster

WHAT AM I TO SAY to you on an occasion like this? It would be all too easy to become sentimental about Ampleforth, and all that it has meant to me since my first arrival in 1933; that would be embarrassing. Or I could take refuge in clichés and pious phrases to mask the deep sadness that I feel at leaving; that, too, would be embarrassing.

No, we are in the presence of God, and that is a serious matter. Since I am talking to the community—monks, many parents, I am happy to say, and boys—it is right for me, I think, to reflect before you on a few things that are foremost in my mind, and take you into my confidence.

I think, first of all, of our Lord's first followers and friends—Peter, Matthew, Paul—how very human they were, what faults they had, and how, humanly speaking, they were quite inadequate for their high calling and the tasks which they were given: to preach the Gospel to all and to be shining examples of all that is best in Christian living. And yet St. Paul could write this (and these words have been ringing in my ears these last six days): 'So much wiser than men is God's foolishness, so much stronger than man's is God's weakness. Consider, brethren, the circumstances of your calling; not many of you are wise in the world's fashion, not many powerful, not many well-born'. And then comes the point—'God has chosen what the world holds foolish, so as to abash the wise, God has chosen what the world holds weak, so as to abash the strong. God has chosen what the world holds contemptible—no, has chosen what is nothing—so as to bring to nothing

190

what is now in being; no human creature was to have any ground for boasting in the presence of God.'[1]

The generosity of the Press, and the expectations of so many people, expressed in over a thousand letters[2] and close on four hundred telegrams, have been to me personally a profound shock. That, my deàrly beloved, is why I need your prayers and your friendship. The gap between what is thought and expected of me, and what I know myself to be, is considerable and frightening. There are moments in life when a man feels very small, and in all my life this is one such moment. It is good to feel small, for I know that whatever I achieve will be God's achievement, not mine.

What of you? There is so much good that each one of you can do. I really do believe that we are on the verge of really understanding what God means, and can mean, to our modern world, and how this can be a source of joy and inspiration in the lives of millions of people. A week ago I could not have said that; now I just know. What a happiness it would be to me to know that all of you in this church felt the same; what good you can do with a whole lifetime before you. What has happened to me must happen to you. I have been raised to higher things in spite of myself; you, too, must be raised to higher things in spite of yourselves. So pause to think; let there be only noble thoughts in your minds, and noble deeds in your actions —let there be nothing mean or petty. The eyes of millions of people are on you as well as on me, for you are Ampleforth, and I am only moving to Westminster because I have been Abbot of Ampleforth. A trick of history sees me as head of this Community of monks, of lay persons who work with us, and of this school. What I am is what you have given. And I have been responsible for a very wonderful Community, but a very human one. I would urge you, insist with you, that you rally round the monastic Community and the lay staff, be their support in the years to come, and especially in the next few months. You need each other, and remember, many will be watching you as they are watching me.

You need each other . . .

---

[1] 1 Cor. 1:25–29.
[2] By the time of the Ordination and Installation five weeks later the Archbishop had received 4,400 letters of congratulation.

Let me add a point: Ampleforth must be a community of love. Christ is saying to us in a special way today (we have just read it in the Gospel): 'This is my commandment, love one another as I have loved you.' And this means endless understanding of each other's frailties, forgiveness, tolerance—all that is fine and noble. 'A man can have no greater love than to lay down his life for his friends,' and everyone in this large community which we call Ampleforth must be a friend to the other. That is not only a divine law, it is the only way to peace and justice, it is the only way to find true happiness. There is no greater betrayal of another than to fail to love him, and one of the most tragic aspects of our modern society is the betrayal of one by another: it is the failure to love. There is too little love in this world of ours, and what a difficult and delicate thing it is to handle; into what pitfalls can we fall. But it is the love of God for us and the love of each other which is at the heart of the Christian message.

Strangely, in these last few days I have found a new confidence in God, and I hope you have too—and I shall depend on complete trust between all of us, you and me, because you are special. I am not going to say 'goodbye'. We shall be working together, and my ideals, I trust, will be yours.

Let St. Paul have the last word: 'Finally, brothers, fill your minds with everything that is true, everything that is noble, everything that is good and pure, everything that we love and honour, and everything that can be thought virtuous or worthy of praise.'[1]

[1] Phil. 4:4–9.